CW01669083

what we mean when we talk about strategy

what we mean
when we talk about

strategy

Stuart Crainer and Des Dearlove

THINKERS 50

A Thinkers50 publication
in association with Infinite Ideas

infinite ideas

First published in 2016 by
Infinite Ideas Limited
36 St Giles
Oxford
OX1 3LD
United Kingdom
www.infideas.com

A CIP catalogue record for this book is available from the British Library
ISBN 978–1–908984–58–6

Printed in Britain by 4edge Limited

Contents

Introduction

Strategy is the capstone of our studies into how leaders and organizations work. It goes in and out of fashion but remains, hovering in the air in every board meeting, lingering with intent as entrepreneurs hatch their bright ideas, and peppering the conversations of the ambitious, bold and sometimes foolhardy wherever they are in the world. Strategy is the intellectual heavy lifting in the business world.

The word strategy derives from the Greek for generalship, strategia, and entered the English vocabulary in 1688 as strategie. According to James' 1810 Military Dictionary, it differs from tactics, which are immediate measures in the face of an enemy. Strategy concerns something 'done out of sight of an enemy'. Its origins are frequently traced back to Sun Tzu's *The Art of War* from 500 BC. However, present-day strategy guru, Gary Hamel says:

> Strategy didn't start with Igor Ansoff [author of *Strategic Management*]; neither did it start with Machiavelli. It probably didn't even start with Sun Tzu. Strategy is as old as human conflict – and if the stakes are high in business, they're rather higher in the military sphere. In fact, one of the best strategy books I've ever read is *Military Misfortune* by two professors of military strategy at America's naval college.

While strategy is timeless, despite centuries of study it remains subject to endless debate. It is, for the most part, a deliciously imprecise and confused art – if, indeed, it is an art at all.

We hope you enjoy this smorgasbord of strategy. It is the fruits of our past two decades writing about business ideas. It does not provide easy answers, but will hopefully encourage you to ask the vital questions to get to your own answers to the strategic challenges you face.

Stuart Crainer and Des Dearlove
September 2016

In search of strategy #1

Always start by defining terms. It sounds sensible and straightforward – especially with a subject like strategy which has been studied from every angle.

But it is not.

In 1987 Henry Mintzberg offered five definitions of strategy for consideration: plan, ploy, pattern, position and perspective. Strategy is perhaps most commonly envisaged as a plan – consciously intended action developed in advance. A related concept is strategy as a ploy – a specific maneuver designed to outfox opponents. Strategy as pattern – the focus of much of Mintzberg's research – is a consistency of behavior intended or otherwise. Strategy can be a position, an organization locating itself in an environment as Mintzberg describes it. This definition of strategy is consistent with the preceding definitions; an organization can position itself via a plan, as plan, or as a pattern of behavior. Finally, suggests Mintzberg, there is strategy as a perspective. In this instance it is effectively the ingrained perspective the organization has, it is a collective and shared outlook on the world.

In *The Financial Times Guide to Strategy*, Richard Koch provides two senses for strategy:

> 1. A good strategy is the commercial logic of a business, that defines why a firm can have a competitive advantage and a place in the sun. To be complete, a strategy must include a definition of the domain – the lines of business, types of customer and geographical reach – in which the firm competes. It must also include a definition of

> the firm's distinctive competencies and the competitive advantage that gives the firm a special hold on the chosen business domain.
>
> 2. Strategy also means what a company does, how it actually positions itself commercially and conducts the competitive battle. You can always attempt to describe a competitor's strategy, whether or not you think it sound. In this sense a strategy is what a firm does, not what it says it does, or what its strategy documents propounded.

This provides some reassuring clarity, but also establishes that the scope of strategy in incredibly broad – from the logic of a business to what it actually does. And, as we shall see, the scope of strategy is ever broadening.

Costas Markides, the charismatic London Business School professor, provides this overview:

> There is general agreement that every company needs a strategy – either explicit or implicit. Yet, there is surprisingly little agreement as to what strategy really is. Within both business and academic circles, it is not easy to identify two people who share the same definition of 'strategy'. Differences in opinion on the content and process of developing strategy are passionately argued. Yet these debates cease to matter when we realize two important points. First, strategy needs to be approached from a variety of perspectives. Second, rather than adopt a single perspective at the expense of all others, good strategies have to achieve a fine balance between seemingly divergent views.
>
> When it comes to strategy, I have found that there are three problem areas of controversy. I believe that sound strategic thinking achieves a fine balance between the arguments surrounding: (1) what constitutes the content and process of strategy, (2) strategy as analysis or creativity and (3) strategy dynamics. Analyzing each area in turn will help in achieving that fine balance.
>
> Strategy is both of these things: strategy must decide what game we want to play and then determine how to play that game well. As

practiced today, strategy is preoccupied with fixing the problems in the existing business rather than thinking about future businesses. The essence of a good strategy is to create new markets, new products and new industries. This leads to the position that strategy should be about competing for the industries of the future rather than competing for market share in the industries of today. It is hard to argue with the need to focus the organization's attention on discovering new markets. But this should not come at the expense of today's businesses.

Therefore, the key question for any company is not whether it should try to create the industries of the future but how to take care of its existing business while at the same time attempting to create the industries of the future. Every company should also prepare for an unknown future — either by trying to create this new future itself or by creating the conditions that would allow it to exploit the future when it unfolds.

As these takes on strategy suggest, strategy really is a moveable feast, an awkward hybrid of delivery in the present and mapping out a persuasive future and a route to get there. The challenge for all those charged with leading organizations is to reach their own definition of what strategy is and what it should do. Without this as a starting point, strategy is as useful as whistling in the organizational wind.

Resources

Richard Koch, *The Financial Times Guide to Strategy*, FT Prentice Hall, 2011.

War material #2

The great business thinker Peter Drucker noted that his book *Managing for Results*, published in 1964, was the 'first book ever on what we now call strategy'. For once, the venerable sage of business might have been overstating his intellectual credentials. Strategy is as old as humanity. But its most coherent lineage lies in the military world. The book commonly taken as the strategic bible is a military one: Sun Tzu's *The Art of War*.

The authorship of *The Art of War* remains, perhaps understandably, clouded in mystery. It may have been written by Sun Wu, a military general who was alive around 500 BC. His book is reputed to have led to a meeting between Sun Wu and King Ho-lü of Wu. Sun Wu, not having a flip chart available, argued his case for military discipline by decapitating two of the king's concubines. The book's actual title is Sun Tzu Ping Fa which can be literally translated as 'The military method of venerable Mr. Sun'.

Military examples and imagery have played an important role in the development of management thinking. Even now, military role models – whether they are Colin Powell or Norman Schwarzkopf – are keenly seized upon by executives. The military, with its elements of strategy and leadership, is alluring and the link between the military and business worlds has existed since time immemorial. Books as diverse as Carl Von Clausewitz's *On War* (1908), B.H. Liddell Hart's *Strategy* (1967) and Miyamoto Mushashi's *The Book of Five Rings* (1974) have explored the link.

Generally, the attraction of the military analogy is that it is clear who your enemy is. When your enemy is clear, the world appears clearer – if you are a military general or a CEO. *The Art of War* is usually interpreted in such terms, as an aggressive counterpoint to the confusion of mere theory. In fact, *The Art of War* is more sophisticated than that. Why destroy when you can win by stealth and cunning? Sun Tzu says:

> A sovereign should not start a war out of anger, nor should a general give battle out of rage. For while anger can revert to happiness and rage to delight, a nation that has been destroyed cannot be restored, nor can the dead be brought back to life. To subdue the enemy's forces without fighting is the summit of skill. The best approach is to attack the other side's strategy; next best is to attack his alliances; next best is to attack his soldiers; the worst is to attack cities.

Sun Tzu also has sound advice on knowing your markets. 'Advance knowledge cannot be gained from ghosts and spirits … but must be obtained from people who know the enemy situation.'

Elsewhere, Sun Tzu lapses into Confucian analogies which would appear to be anathema to hard-headed modern executives. Often, however, they appear to find them reassuring:

> For the shape of an army is like that of water. The shape of water is to avoid heights and flow towards low places; the shape of the army is to avoid strength and to strike at weakness. Water flows in accordance with the ground; an army achieves victory in accordance with the enemy.

But, *The Art of War* is best known as the origin of the concept of strategy, one that has been through a great many reinterpretations in the intervening 2,500 years. Here, there is no room for sentiment or distraction:

> Deploy forces to defend the strategic points; exercise vigilance in preparation, do not be indolent. Deeply investigate the true situation, secretly await their laxity. Wait until they leave their strongholds, then seize what they love.

It is plain and simple, but brutal, a lot like warfare.

The simplicity of the strategy-as-warfare metaphor is alluring. But many modern-day strategists question its implications. For example, Renée Mauborgne, co-author of the strategy blockbuster *Blue Ocean Strategy* offers an alternative perspective:

> The essence of business strategy can be traced to military strategy. That's why traditionally the field of strategy talked about headquarters rather than head office. In terrain and war there's only so much land that exists. Fundamentally that explains why business strategy – including competitive strategy – has been predominantly based on how you divide up an existing pie. It's about relative power. It's a zero sum game because you cannot multiply the size of land available.
>
> The question is: why has the field of business strategy sometimes implicitly, sometimes explicitly taken this assumption to be true? While strategy in war may be limited to dividing up existing non-changeable land masses, if there is one thing the world has taught us over the last 100 years it is that in the realm of business the new market spaces that can be created are infinite. What you see if you look historically is that real gains came when people created an entirely new area – a whole new market space. You can create a win:win game. You can create new land. Just think of the number of industries that exist today that did not exist even thirty years prior. Scientifically we know the same amount of chemical compounds that exist has not changed over time. But look at what you had in the beginning – just dinosaurs. And today by creatively combining them in numerous new ways we have … Starbucks. What we can buy today in a Seven Eleven store beats what a king like Louis XIV had. The possibilities are endless.

Indeed they are, but having Sun Tzu in your pocket is still attractive. It is the nuclear option for strategy, destructive rather than creative, but undeniably powerful.

Resources

Sun Tzu, *The Art of War*, Pax Liborum, 2009.
Carl von Clausewitz, *On War*, Oxford University Press, 2008.

Simply, strategy #3

Sometimes you read of a strategic move and its simplicity has a brutal beauty. Some entrepreneurs and, perhaps fewer executive leaders, can lay claim to doing something truly original, executing a new and novel strategy. Often these are based on simple, old fashioned notions.

Decide to cut out the extras and focus on what you can deliver and what the customer really wants. How many companies can honestly say that they have made that decision? Herb Kelleher at Southwest Airlines can.

Southwest stamped an indelible mark on the airline industry. It is the godfather of the likes of Ryanair and easyJet. Herb Kelleher proved that differentiation is a CEO-level issue. 'It is still the low-cost airline by which all others are judged,' notes the *Financial Times*.

Yet, if you look at the basics, Southwest doesn't appear to have a lot going for it. Its product is, from a business person's perspective, plainly inferior. There is no first class, no seat assignment. This is the kind of thing that matters to harried business people anxious to finish a report on their laptop during the flight. Yet, Southwest still captures a reasonable share of business traffic. Its services are high frequency, punctual, and passengers have shorter ground journeys as Southwest flies to alternative airports. The value of this higher certainty and shorter overall door-to-door time is immeasurable to many business travelers. On top of this is the legendary, much talked about, Southwest service which is built around people enjoying their work and enjoying helping customers. Southwest started wooing customers – male ones at least – with a

'Love' theme (drinks became Love Potions). Now, it does so through its promise of 'positively outrageous service'.

In a business that is often bland, Southwest sends out strong, simple messages to customers and employees and this adds value for both groups. This information flow combines to help the company's logistics. Turnaround times tend to be quicker than those of competitors – often 20 minutes – because staff work together. There is a similar win-win in the company's use of a standardized fleet of Boeing 737s. A single plane means a single inventory of spare parts. Customers don't care if it is a 737 so long as it gets them to their destination safely and on time.

> The end product of strategic decisions is deceptively simple; a combination of products and markets is selected for the firm. This combination is arrived at by addition of new product-markets, divestment from some old ones, and expansion of the present position.
>
> **Igor Ansoff, strategy guru**

It is nothing like rocket science. But it gave Southwest a huge headstart. It invented a new channel – low thrills, low cost, high service – and, as a result, captured the Texan market and built up a tidy cash pile to expand into other plum markets such as California. Southwest built up a long record of uninterrupted in the black performance.

Others have, inevitably, boarded the bandwagon. But, achieving such strategic clarity is easier said than done. The lesson from Southwest is to keep it simple. Strategy needs to be compellingly straightforward in order for it to be understood and executed effectively. Another airline exec who understood Kelleher's message was Gordon Bethune, when chairman and CEO of Continental Airlines. He took on the job in 1994. It didn't appear to be the greatest career move. In fact, it appeared to be the career-equivalent of suicide. Continental was in disastrously bad shape. The previous CEO Frank Lorenzo had followed a cheap fare strategy which had got the airline nowhere. It had been in Chapter 11 and seemed stuck in the red. Its market capitalization of $230 million was actually less than the trade-in value of its planes. (This must rank as one of the most inglorious achievements in recent managerial history.) Continental lost $204 million in 1994.

Things were bad. 'We even had pilots turning down the air conditioning and slowing down planes to save the cost of fuel. They made passengers hot, mad, and late,' said Bethune.

On arrival Bethune took the double locks off the executive offices on the twentieth floor. He ordered that the planes be repainted so that they were all the same color. He instructed staff to ensure that the planes were cleaned three times more often. He announced that every month that Continental was in the top five airlines in on-time performance everyone got $65 – the company lost $6 million per month by being late. In the first month Continental was seventh; in the second it was fourth and in the third, first.

In 1996 Continental made profits of $556 million. *Fortune* selected it as the Most Improved Company of the 1990s. 'We don't spend a lot of time on strategy; we spend more time on implementation, making sure we get it done,' said Bethune who – like Herb Kelleher – proved single-handedly that strategy is not aeronautic science: great strategy is simple.

Resources

Kevin and Jackie Freiberg, *Nuts!*, Texere, 2001.
Jody Hoffer Gittell, *The Southwest Airlines Way*, McGraw Hill, 2005.

The mighty Porter #4

In his speech accepting his award for topping the 2015 Thinkers50 ranking, Michael Porter told us:

> Ideas truly do change the world. I have seen that with my own eyes all throughout my career. I also believe that management thinking unlocks value in every field not just business. We all understand that management thinking allows markets to work better in delivering value to customers. We have also learned that management thinking and deeply understanding competition at the grassroots level reveal the true sources of competitiveness and what really leads to economic development. This is starting to permeate its way through our economic development thinking.
>
> Based on my recent work, management thinking unlocks value in health care. Medical science is not the constraint in health care today, it is the ability to think strategically, to organize, to measure the right way, to create new kinds of delivery systems. I also think management thinking and a new conception of how corporations relate to society is one of the most powerful tools we have in the world to address society's pressing challenges.

Porter of Harvard Business School is probably the world's most successful academic. While other management thinkers have compromised their approach in search of popular appeal, Porter's seriousness and rationality is all pervasive. 'His work is academic almost to a fault,' observed *The Economist*. 'Mr Porter is about as likely to produce a blockbuster full of anecdotes and boosterish catch-phrases as he is to deliver a lecture dressed in bra and stockings.'

His approach is based on surgical precision, the dissection of the vital organs of companies and industrial nations. Porter's books, not surprisingly, have been few in number, but high in their ambition and influence.

'Strategic thinking rarely occurs spontaneously. Without guidelines few managers knew what constituted strategic thinking,' he lamented in a 1987 article. His work has set about constructing the guidelines.

Porter's first book was *Competitive Strategy* (1980) which instead of tiptoeing round the edges of management theory went straight to the strategic heart. Porter tackled the apparently imponderable question of how organizations can achieve long-term competitive advantage. He sought a middle ground between the two polarized approaches then accepted – on the one hand, that competitive advantage was achieved by organizations adapting to their particular circumstances; and, on the other, that competitive advantage was based on the simple principle that the more in-tune and aware of a market a company is, the more competitive it can be (through lower prices and increased market share).

Porter managed to absorb both these concepts. From analysis of a number of companies, he developed generic strategies. This was not an instant template for competitive advantage – Porter insisted that though the generic strategies existed, it was up to each organization to carefully select which were most appropriate to them and at which particular time. The four generic strategies are backed by five competitive forces which are then applied to five 'different kinds of industries' (fragmented, emerging, mature, declining and global). The logic behind the five forces framework is that:

- If customers have bargaining power over a supplier (no matter what the reason), they will exercise that power and reduce the supplier's profit margins.

- If an organization's suppliers have bargaining power over it, they will exercise that power and sell their products at a higher price.

- If there are substitutes to an organization's product or service, they will limit the price the organization can charge and, again, limit profits.

- If there is intense rivalry in an industry, it will force organizations to engage in price, R&D and advertising wars, all of which are likely to reduce profits.

- Finally, if new entrants move into an industry, they bring with them resources and the desire to steal market share from existing companies. Rivalry accelerates and profits decline.

London Business School's Costas Markides says:

> Given the logic of these five forces, a strategist needs to decide what to do about them. Traditionally, most people assumed that the way to proceed was to assume these five industry forces as given and then try and position their firm towards these forces. This is fundamentally wrong and this is probably the most serious misconception about strategy that has developed since the five forces framework was developed.

Markides argues that what the strategist ought to do is to creatively break the established rules of the game by actively changing these five forces in the company's favor. In his view, the essence of strategy formulation is coming up with creative ideas in response to the following five questions:

- How can I reduce the bargaining power of my customers?

- How can I reduce the bargaining power of my suppliers?

- How can I reduce substitutes to my product or service?

- How can I limit rivalry in my industry?

- How can I prevent new entrants from coming into my industry?

Taught at every business school in the world, Porter's generic strategies framework is persuasive and highly attractive to managers. It is clear and the logic irrefutable. The trouble is that, while Porter suggests that the model should only be used to stimulate thinking, organizations often regard it as a direct route to competitive advantage. There is considerable irony in companies using the same model to differentiate themselves from each other.

Later, in *Competitive Advantage* (1985) Porter went on to contend that there are three ways by which companies can gain competitive advantage:

- by becoming the lowest cost producer in a given market;

- by being a differentiated producer (offering something extra or special to charge a premium price);

- or by being a focused producer (achieving dominance in a niche market).

To examine an organization's internal competitiveness, Porter advocates the use of a value chain – analysis of a company's internal processes and the interactions between different elements of the organization to determine how and where value is added. Viewing everything a company does in terms of its overall competitiveness, argues Porter, is a crucial step to becoming more competitive.

Porter went on to paint on a bigger canvas. *The Competitive Advantage of Nations* (1990), one of his most ambitious projects, is a detailed study of the competitiveness of the world's top eight economies which emerged from Porter's work on the Presidential Commission on Industrial Competitiveness set up by Ronald Reagan. Interestingly, Porter produces a more pragmatic view of the world in this book. He is highly critical of general prescriptions and the worldwide application of management fads such as just-in-time. What works in one country, fails miserably in another, he warns. This runs counter to much of the prevailing wisdom of globalization. Indeed, instead of national differences and characteristics becoming less pronounced, Porter found them to be as important as ever.

Again, Porter's research produced a tidy checklist. His national diamond framework identified four factors which influence the competitiveness of nations:

- Resources,
- Related and supporting industries,
- Demanding home customers,
- Domestic rivalry.

While Porter has attracted some criticism for his willingness to boil his mass of theories and ideas down to all-embracing bullet-points, without them it is unlikely that his complex ideas would either be accessible or understood. That they are so influential is a triumph for Porter's abilities of dissection and logic.

Resources

Michael Porter's books include *Competitive Strategy*, Free Press, 1980; *Competitive Advantage*, Free Press, 1985; and *The Competitive Advantage of Nations*, Macmillan, 1990.
'Professor Porter PhD', *The Economist*, 8 October 1994.

Key questions #5

At the heart of strategy is the ability to create a plan of action which will lead to victory – whatever victory is thought to be in this instance. But, before the strategy is created a more basic question needs to be asked. In *The Mind of the Strategist* Kenichi Ohmae explains:

> The strategist's method is very simply to challenge the prevailing assumptions with a single question: Why? and to put the same question relentlessly to those responsible for the current way of doing things until they are sick of it.

Before setting off it is worth returning to first principles and asking some vital questions.

Where are you?

The starting point must be a solid understanding of where you are starting from and the dilemmas you face. If organizations are not in touch with the reality of their situation – however depressing this may seem – they have no hope of moving forward.

Where do you want to be?

If you don't know where you want to be you are unlikely to get there.

In pursuit of this starting point organizations throughout the world have developed mission statements. 'Most companies do have a mission statement. About 99.9 percent are useless,' observes Costas Markides of London Business School. Mission statements are also, confusingly, known by a variety of other labels (strategic intent, core objectives, visions, etc.) but the end-result is usually remarkably similar. Blandness does not differentiate or motivate.

Mission statements are, or should be, a pithy explanation of why a company is in business, what it intends to achieve and by what methods. The exercise of distilling an organization's *raison d'être* into less than 100 words is often useful in itself. However, the results are often fatuous in the extreme. Mission statements have become meaningless PR exercises, pinned on noticeboards, printed on corporate keepsakes and generally ignored by the people they aim to influence. 'Many managers misunderstand the nature and importance of mission, while others fail to comprehend it at all,' concluded Andrew Campbell and his co-authors in *A Sense of Mission*.

> One person's strategy is another's tactics.
>
> **Anon**

Though they might help to encapsulate an organization's goals, mission statements are not strategy. They are more accurately described as the potential end-result of strategy, the objectives of the organization. Indeed, Henry Mintzberg defines strategy as the embodiment of a company's visions.

Mission statements should be bold, but achievable, goals. It sounds straightforward, but the means of identifying these objectives is clouded by controversy.

What do you want to achieve?

Any statement of intent relies on some knowledge of what it is you wish to achieve. Michael Porter argues that what every company should aim to achieve is competitive advantage. It must be better than its competitors in some way.

This has led to the elusive and almost mythical notion of sustainable competitive advantage. (One of the most important strategy books of the past decade, by Columbia Business School's Rita McGrath, is entitled *The End of Competitive Advantage*.) In reality, any competitive advantage is short-lived. If a company raises its quality standards and increases profits as a result, its competitors will follow. Businesses are quick to copy, mimic, pretend and, even, steal.

The logical and distressing conclusion is that an organization has to be continuously developing new forms of competitive advantage. It must move on all the time. If it stands still, competitive advantage will evaporate before its very eyes and competitors will pass.

The dangers of developing continuously are that it generates, and relies on, a climate of uncertainty. The company also runs the risk of fighting on too many fronts. This is often manifested in a huge number of improvement programs in various parts of the organization which give the impression of moving forward, but are often simply cosmetic.

Constantly evolving and developing strategy is called strategic innovation. The mistake is to assume that strategic innovation calls for radical and continual major surgery on all corporate arteries. Continuous small changes across an organization make a difference. 'We did not seek to be 100 percent better at anything. We seek to be one percent better at 100 things,' said Jan Carlzon when he was CEO of the airline SAS.

What needs to change?

Even major surgery has its compromises. More realistic than most, the Japanese strategist Kenichi Ohmae, says that a good business strategy 'is one, by which a company can gain significant ground on its competitors at an acceptable cost to itself'. He believes there are four principal ways of doing this:

1. Focus on the key factors for success (KFSs). Ohmae argues that certain functional or operating areas within every business are more critical for success in that particular business environment than others. If you concentrate effort into these areas and your competitors do not, this is a source of competitive advantage. The problem, of course,

is identifying what these key factors for success are.

2. Build on relative superiority. When all your competitors are seeking to compete on the KFSs, a company can exploit any differences in competitive conditions. For example, it can make use of technology or sales networks not in direct competition with its rivals.

3. Pursue aggressive initiatives. Frequently, the only way to win against a much larger, entrenched competitor is to upset the competitive environment, by undermining the value of its KFSs – changing the rules of the game by introducing new KFSs.

4. Utilizing strategic degrees of freedom. By this tautological phrase, Ohmae means that the company can focus on innovation in areas which are 'untouched by competitors'.

'In each of these four methods, the principal concern is to avoid doing the same thing, on the same battleground, as the competition,' Ohmae explains.

What are you good at?

The phrase core competencies has now entered the language of management. In layman's terms, core competencies are what a company excels at.

Gary Hamel and C.K. Prahalad, who made the term famous, define core competencies as 'the skills that enable a firm to deliver a fundamental customer benefit'. Hamel and Prahalad argue that strategic planning is neither radical enough nor sufficiently long term in perspective. Instead its aim remains incremental improvement. In contrast, they advocate crafting strategic architecture. The phraseology is unwieldy, but means basically that organizations should concentrate on rewriting the rules of their industry.

What is the context?

Nothing in the corporate world exists in a vacuum. Formulating a mission or any set of objectives must involve a plethora of people, as well as consideration of the broader forces at work in and on the organization.

This process was neatly summed up by Peter Drucker in a 1994 *Harvard Business Review* article. Drucker argues that every organization has a theory of business – the assumptions on which it has been built and is being run. To create a 'valid theory of business' requires four elements:

1. The assumptions about environment, mission and core competencies must fit reality.
2. The assumptions in all three areas have to fit one another.
3. The theory of the business must be known and understood throughout the organization.
4. The theory of the business has to be tested constantly.

Along similar lines, Kenichi Ohmae argues that an effective strategic plan takes account of three main players – the company, the customer and the competition – each exerting their own influence. The strategy that ignores competitive reaction is flawed; so is the strategy that does not take into account sufficiently how the customer will react; and so, of course, is the strategic plan that does to explore fully the organization's capacity to implement it.

How do you achieve your objectives?

Implementation is where most strategies fail. Success relies on matching an organization's resources, culture, structure and people to the strategies which emerge from consideration of an organization's core competencies and the environment it exists in.

Of course, no list of questions provides a foolproof answer or set of answers. The challenge for any organization is to develop its own culture of asking questions and interrogating reality. Passive acceptance is the route to failure; robust, continual questioning the path to strategic success.

Resources

Gary Hamel and C.K. Prahalad, *Competing for the Future*, Harvard Business School Press, 1994.

Costas Markides, *Diversification, Refocusing and Economic Performance*, MIT Press, 1995.

J.I. Moore, *Writers on Strategy and Strategic Management*, Penguin, 1992.

Kenichi Ohmae, *The Mind of the Strategist*, McGraw Hill, 1982.

Strategy at work #6

In 1987 Wal-Mart decided to move into the grocery business. In doing so it changed the grocery industry and provided the foundations for its explosive growth throughout the 1990s.

In the late 1980s, Wal-Mart was eyeing Europe with increasing interest. Europe was experiencing a boom in hypermarkets. This format had been started by the European retailer, Carrefour in 1962. By 1988 it ran 73 hypermarkets throughout Europe and, overall, there were 780. The idea behind hypermarkets was straightforward: the stores sold grocery and other general goods under one extremely large roof. Customers could load up with their week's groceries and buy some clothes or household items at the same time.

Some US chains already offered both groceries and general merchandise. The potential for Wal-Mart, the dominant general merchandise retailer, was clear. A combined merchandise/grocery operation offered the chance to continue the company's rapid expansion. At the time, Wal-Mart controlled 50 percent of the $150 billion discount store business. Another 32 percent of the industry was controlled by K-mart and Target. Any further inroads into market share were going to be difficult to achieve.

Grocery retailing, in contrast, was alluring. Wal-Mart saw that this $400 billion industry was extremely intriguing – and fragmented. The largest supermarket chain, Krogers, controlled a mere 6 percent of the market and the top ten combined only mustered 19 percent of the market.

The downside of grocery retailing was simply that margins were low. Expansion was possible but focused grocery outlets would always be

> Strategy is extraordinarily emotional and demanding. It is not a ritual or a once-a-year exercise, though that is what it has become. We have set the bar too low.
>
> **Gary Hamel**

handicapped by the industry's poor margins. But, looked at differently, Wal-Mart saw a more positive message – consumers visit grocery stores more regularly than general merchandise stores; if the opportunity was there for customers to cross the aisle and buy some general merchandise, the conundrum of low margins in the grocery business and intense competition in general merchandising could be solved.

In 1987 Wal-Mart tested the water with Hypermart USA. It brought in grocery experts and brought some grocery companies in as partners – this culminated in the 1991 purchase of McLane & Co, a grocery and general merchandise wholesaler.

The first Hypermarts provided a variety of lessons. These were taken on board when Wal-Mart opened its first Supercenter in Washington, MO in March 1988. The new store was smaller than the Hypermart format. More followed. Over the next two years, five more Supercenters were built in Missouri, Oklahoma and Arkansas. The smallest was 90,000 square feet; the biggest 170,000.

With six Supercenters and four Hypermarts up and running, the piloting process was underway so that Wal-Mart could fully understand the potential business proposition and likely problems in introducing the combo format. One notable challenge was posed by inventory. Wal-Mart was used to carrying a full 60 days of inventory in general merchandising. In the grocery business, 25 days of inventory was normal – less than 10 days for meat and other fresh produce. In response, Wal-Mart increased its inventory management capabilities and created manufacturing systems in certain areas.

It took four years of experimentation before Wal-Mart took the plunge into Supercenters. Between 1992 and 1998, it built 558 such stores. Roll out was rapid. Every single store built on the lessons learned in the pilot phase of the early 1990s.

The end result was that by 1998 Wal-Mart had grocery sales of $32 billion and was the third largest supermarket operator – becoming the largest early in the new century. The mutually beneficial relationship between grocery and general merchandise was largely confirmed – Superstores had 30 percent greater general merchandise sales than their discount store counterparts.

And the strategic lessons? Put your toes in the water, not your legs. Wal-Mart experimented and tried the hypermarket format in a limited number of locations. The stores were enormous – 220,000 square feet – complex, costly and made small profits, but they were important sources of learning – and, most importantly, learning which the company acted on.

Piloting strategy makes sense – as it makes sense in developing products and services. One of the champions of this approach is Roger Martin who worked with the legendary A.G. Lafley at Procter & Gamble. Martin and Lafley were influenced by the idea of design thinking which uses pilots and prototypes. Martin told us:

> A.G. and I are both really interested in the world of design. You prototype your strategy decision, and then you look back and, based on what's happened when we've exposed the prototype to people, we say, oh, you know, that's sort of right, but not quite. And you have that attitude towards strategy, so it doesn't feel like failure, it feels like getting it better and better and better.

An even bigger point here is picked up by Rita McGrath who points to the convergence of the worlds of strategy and innovation:

> When I started my professional career innovation was over there, that weird thing that the creative people did, and strategy was over here and all about positioning and markets and so forth. Now they're converging. So one of the things I argue that companies need to get better at is developing what I call innovation proficiency. And what that involves is having funds for it, having a governing mechanism for it, having people who actually do it for a living. It used to be innovation was always a great job but a lousy career.
>
> What we're going to see now is companies actually building out

> that capability in a very systematic way. So the Australian logistics company, Brambles, which has a really exciting business; they were founded on the basis of thousands of pallets left behind by the armored troops after World War Two in Australia, and they get paid for shipping these pallets all around the world. Now, you wouldn't think a company like that would be a hotbed of innovation and yet they've really turned it into a systemic capability.
>
> What they've realized is that one of the biggest barriers to innovation for a P&L manager is the risk of trying something new that backfires. So, what do you do if it doesn't work? The worry is that it's going to show up in my numbers, it's going to make me look bad. So what the CEO has done is he's actually allocated funds in such a way that if the business succeeds the P&L manager gets all the credit, but if it doesn't work out corporate takes the hit. And so as a consequence, instead of the usual managers' response, which is, oh, I don't want those innovation things, they're too risky, they're like, bring it on, bring it on, give me as many as you can because it's only upside.

The message is simple: try something small and if it backfires, think again.

The second strategic lesson is even simpler: take control. Why dilute your control by involving others? If you have the financial muscle, take control. Wal-Mart developed its own food distribution network – rather than relying on other distributors; and its engineers and construction team learned from grocery store professionals how to construct stores which were suitable to this new use and cheaper than those built by the competition. Test marketing continues even now so that learning and improvement are on-going.

Blue, blue oceans #7

The strategy battle rumbles on. Those in search of strategic inspiration are faced with two alternatives. Either, they start with their industry as the basic strategic building block (Michael Porter's Five Forces), or with their company (Gary Hamel and C.K. Prahalad's core competencies). Over the last three decades a great deal of intellectual energy has been expended on refining these two worldviews. But other ideas are also coming to the fore. W. Chan Kim and Renée Mauborgne, based at INSEAD, the leading European business school, just south of Paris, challenge the strategy orthodoxy.

'There's no such thing as a permanently great company or a permanently great industry. All industries rise and fall as do companies,' they explain. 'However, there are permanently smart strategic moves.'

Kim and Mauborgne's reputation is built around a series of acclaimed articles in the *Harvard Business Review* and the bestselling book, *Blue Ocean Strategy*. Their work is supported by a substantial database – a database that now extends all the way back to 1850.

So what does all this data show? Kim and Mauborgne believe that the business world has been overlooking one of the key lessons of wealth creation in history. Their research indicates that the major source of wealth creation over time is not the industry that a company plays in per se. Nor did they find permanently great companies that consistently captured wealth. (This contradicts books like *In Search of Excellence* and *Built to Last*, which seek to distill the characteristics of great companies). Instead they found that an industry's and a company's ups and

> Self-generated strategic change requires the stamina, the endurance and the resilience to just keep coming back to that strategy. You get knocked partly off, but you come back again. You get knocked the other way off, but you come back. You're not going to arrive if you get diverted.
>
> **Allen Sheppard, British executive**

downs are substantially attributable to something they call strategic moves.

'By strategic move we mean the actions of players in conceiving, launching, and realizing their business ideas. In each strategic move, there are winners, losers, and mere survivors,' says Mauborgne.

A snapshot of the auto-industry from 1900 to 1940 is instructive. As Kim and Mauborgne articulate, 'Ford's Model T, launched in 1908, triggered the industry's growth and profitability, replacing the horse-drawn carriage with the car for American households. It lifted Ford's market share from 9 to 60 percent.'

The Model T, then, was the strategic move that ignited the automotive industry. But in 1924, it was overtaken by another move, this time by GM. Kim explains:

> Contrary to Ford's functional one-colour one-car single model strategy, GM created the new market space of emotional stylized cars with 'a car for every purpose and purse'. Not only was the auto industry's growth and profitability again catapulted to new heights, but GM's market share jumped from 20 to 50 percent while Ford's fell from 60 to 20 percent.

Over the 150-year period, they found a similar pattern in other sectors. In short, the strategic move that matters most to both an industry's long-term profitable growth and that of individual companies is the repeated creation over time of new market space that embraces the mass market. Kim and Mauborgne call this 'value innovation'. Without it, whole industries fade into the sunset and are replaced by those which are more innovative. Without it, companies become irrelevant or are overtaken – as Ford was overtaken by GM in the 1920s.

Kim says:

> Value innovation occurs across industries, across countries, across companies. It is a universal force. A company, therefore, substantially limits its strategic opportunities and profitable growth potential by narrowly confining its analysis to its own industry. Yet, in most strategy literature, industry boundaries are regarded as central – think of SWOT analysis or Michael Porter's Five Forces.

According to the blue ocean duo, value innovators differed across five main dimensions of strategy:

1. Industry assumptions: Value innovators assume that they are able to alter and shape industry conditions.

2. Strategic Focus: Instead of responding to rivals, letting their rivals set the parameters for competing, and offering something similar but better, value innovators reinvent markets making great leaps in the value offered.

3. Customers: Rather than focus on segmentation and customization to further refine differing customer needs, value innovators concentrate on customer commonalties among the mass of buyers.

4. Assets and capabilities: Value innovators are not contained by viewing business opportunities through existing assets and capabilities, they frequently take a clean slate approach to create new value.

5. Product and service offerings: Conventional companies operate within a space defined by the products and services that their industry traditionally offers. Value innovators, however, will look for customer solution that they can meet right across the value chain even if that means entering a new business.

Kim and Mauborgne cite the rise of Cemex to become one of the world's largest cement producers as an example of what they are talking about. Cemex created new market space in Mexico by transforming cement into an emotional product.

Mexican houses are traditionally built in stages, a room at a time. This can take many years. Spare cash is often spent on weddings or on relatively expensive gifts for important religious festivities. Realizing this, Cemex has rewritten the rules by repositioning cement as an emotional product – 'the stuff of dreams'.

If you really love somebody, the strategy suggests, cement is the best gift you can give them because you are giving them a home. With a strategic flourish, a flat industry has been transformed into a growth industry where the price of cement jumped from an historical low of some $40/ton to over $100/ton by the late 1990s. By 2002, the *Financial Times* had ranked Cemex as the most admired company in Latin America.

Along similar lines, Kim and Mauborgne note, the coffee industry was dead, until Starbucks came along and kick-started it.

Rather than viewing strategy as enacted in a landscape of dominant companies or industries, Kim and Mauborgne paint a persuasive picture of a commercial world in constant flux, where whole industries rise and then often disappear into oblivion. Says Kim:

> Look back to the major industries of 1970 and very few, if any, are now significant. The big growth industries in the past 30 years have been the computer industry, software, gas-fired electricity plants, cell phones, and the café bar concept. But in 1970 not one of those industries existed in a meaningful way, and that's just 30 years back. The pattern continues as you dig into the past. The big industries of 1940 aren't those of 1910 and so on. We have a hugely underestimated capacity to create new industries.

This, then, is their big discovery. The number of industries is ever expanding – and the pace is accelerating. The implications for chief executives and their advisors are profound. 'What we see is that over a 30 year cycle the focus of commerce, where the money is made, shifts 100 percent,' says Kim. 'Some industries die, some persist. But new industries are constantly being created. It is like a galaxy of stars – infinite.'

In this view the challenge of strategy becomes one of exploration – to discover new markets and new industries. The trouble is that the basis of strategic thinking – and the consulting industry it has spawned – is based on coming up with strategies based on what you can see now. Business strategy is historically intertwined with military notions of strategy. General principles were extracted from the likes of Carl von Clausewitz, a Prussian general, and Sun Tzu, an ancient Chinese theorist, and are still cited as inspirations by the world's managers. This notion of strategy, say Kim and Mauborgne encourages managers to see strategy as a series of battles to be conducted on a neatly defined battlefield. The victor gains ownership of more of the battlefield.

For strategists the choice is to continue to fight battles in what Kim and Mauborgne label the red ocean of competition or to seek their own industry-redefining strategic move into the competitor-free blue ocean.

Resources

W. Chan Kim and Renée Mauborgne, *Blue Ocean Strategy*, Harvard Business School Press, 2005.

Essential thinkers on strategy #8

Richard D'Aveni

Few thinkers manage to change the vocabulary of their area of study and then influence it for decades. Richard D'Aveni has done just that in the sphere of strategy. His career has roamed as widely as his ever-curious intellect.

The starting point for D'Aveni was the book *Hypercompetition*, which established the term in the strategic vocabulary and became a highly influential bestseller.

Since then he has set about reinventing strategy with a focus on using rapid maneuvering rather than defensive barriers. More Sun Tzu than Michael Porter, D'Aveni advocates temporary advantages and the constant disruption of rivals.

His books focus on creating new tools, frameworks and maps that help firms and governments define their playing fields and determine their positioning using spheres of influence. They include *Strategic Supremacy* and *Beating the Commodity Trap*.

D'Aveni has gone on to apply his concepts to the very notion of capitalism and what he sees as the hypercompetition which now exists between nations. These ideas are captured in *Strategic Capitalism*.

Most recently, in a series of influential articles, D'Aveni has charted the rise of 3-D printing and its likely impact on the world of manufacturing.

A professor of strategy at the Tuck School of Business at Dartmouth College, Richard D'Aveni works with Fortune 500 companies as well as governments and some of the world's wealthiest families. His classes are notable for the involvement of some of America's leading CEOs.

Pankaj Ghemawat

Pankaj Ghemawat is the Global Professor of Management and Strategy and Director of the Center for the Globalization of Education and Management at the Stern School of Business, and the Anselmo Rubiralta Professor of Global Strategy at IESE Business School. Prior to that he was the youngest full professor at Harvard Business School. His 2011 book *World 3.0* (Harvard Business Review Press, 2011) won the Thinkers50 Book Award.

Ghemawat's books include *Commitment* (Harvard Business Review Press, 1991); *Games Businesses Play* (Harvard Business Review Press, 1997); *Strategy and the Business Landscape* (Harvard Business Review Press, 1999); and *Redefining Global Strategy* (Harvard Business Review Press, 2007).

IBM chairman and CEO Sam Palmisano described *Redefining Global Strategy* as:

> … an important strategic guidebook for leaders of the 21st century globally integrated enterprise … [with an] analytic framework that is both visionary and pragmatic – aware of the broader historic trajectories of globalization, but grounded in the real kinds of decisions business leaders have to make.

A review in *The Economist* observed that: '*World 3.0* should be read by anyone who wants to understand the most important economic development of our time.'

Pascal Lamy, Director General of the World Trade Organization said that it offered 'recommendations that should inspire all global stakeholders in times of major global challenges'; and Peter Löscher, CEO of Siemens called it 'the right book at the right time ... [about] ways to make the global economy more stable – and more sustainable'.

Ghemawat was nominated for the 2013 Thinkers50 Global Solutions Award for his DHL Global Connectedness Index, a comprehensive analysis of globalization and the rise of emerging markets. He has written more than 100 research articles and case studies, is one of the world's best-selling authors of teaching cases and fellow of the Academy of International Business and of the Strategic Management Society.

Vijay Govindarajan

Vijay Govindarajan is an internationally recognized expert on business strategy, globalization and innovation. While working as the first-ever Professor in Residence and Chief Innovation Consultant at General Electric, he pioneered the concept of Reverse Innovation to describe innovations first adopted in the developing world.

The article he co-authored on the concept with GE's CEO Jeff Immelt and Chris Trimble won the McKinsey Award for Best Article and was chosen by the *Harvard Business Review* as one of the great moments in management of the last century.

Govindarajan is also responsible for posing the question that sparked a global challenge to build a $300 house, which earned him the Thinkers50 C.K. Prahalad Breakthrough Idea Award in 2011. In 2013, he was shortlisted for the Thinkers50 Innovation Award.

More than a quarter of the CEOs and top management teams in the Fortune 500 have invited Govindarajan to work with them on strategy issues. His clients include Boeing, Coca-Cola, Colgate, Deere, FedEx, GE, Hewlett-Packard, IBM, J.P. Morgan Chase, Johnson & Johnson, *New York Times*, Proctor & Gamble, Sony, and Wal-Mart.

His book *Reverse Innovation* (with Chris Trimble) is a *New York Times* and *Wall Street Journal* bestseller.

His most recent book is *The Three Box Solution* (2016). In it, he argues that companies need to master three boxes: box 1. Managing the present, box 2. Selectively forgetting the past, and box 3. Creating the future. Most remain stuck in box 1.

Govindarajan is the Cox Distinguished Professor at Dartmouth College's Tuck School of Business. After training as an accountant in India, he earned a Ph.D. from Harvard Business School.

Anil K. Gupta

There are a great many speakers and pontificators on globalization. Anil K. Gupta lives it. 'Ultimately, strategy is social science, not abstract mathematics; therefore, you need to a have a pretty good understanding of the real world,' he says.

Originally from India where he worked for Unilever, he studied at Harvard Business School and then worked with Vijay Govindarajan on globalization and global strategy – resulting in the book, *The Quest for Global Dominance*.

Since then Anil Gupta's work has embraced the emergence of China as well as that of India. He is chairman of The China India Institute, a Washington DC-based research and consulting organization. His books examining strategies to succeed in the emerging markets include *Getting China and India Right* (winner of the Axiom Book Awards' Silver Prize as one of the world's two best books on globalization/international business); *Global Strategies for Emerging Asia*; and *Smart Globalization*.

His most recent book (co-authored with Haiyan Wang) is *The Silk Road Rediscovered: How Indian and Chinese Companies are Becoming Globally Stronger by Competing in Each Other's Markets*.

Now a professor at the Smith School of Business, at the University of Maryland, Gupta's current research looks at the factors and dynamics which make Silicon Valley the world's pre-eminent innovation center. Perhaps appropriately, he describes himself as 'an intellectual entrepreneur'.

Gupta (www.anilkgupta.com) is an elected member of the board of directors of Origene Technologies (a gene cloning company). He has been on the boards of a number of companies.

Roger Martin

Roger Martin is one of the world's leading authorities on innovation and strategy. He is best known for his work on integrative thinking, and design thinking, both concepts he helped to originate and develop.

Integrative thinking is the ability to balance two opposing ideas or models in order to create a third, more effective solution to a problem. Design Thinking combines analysis and intuition to exploit existing knowledge and create new knowledge.

Martin's pioneering work with A.G. Lafley, CEO at Procter & Gamble, is documented in their best-selling 2013 book *Playing to Win: How Strategy Really Works*. The book sets out a highly practical, step-by-step process for creating a workable business strategy, and explains how the methodology was used to stunning effect, with real life examples at P&G. The book earned Martin and Lafley the 2013 Thinkers50 Distinguished Achievement Award for Best Book.

Martin's other best-sellers include *The Opposable Mind: How Successful Leaders Win Through Integrative Thinking* (2008), *The Design of Business: Why Design Thinking is the Next Competitive Advantage* (2009), and *Fixing the Game: Bubbles, Crashes and What Capitalism Can Learn from the NFL* (2011).

Martin's most recent book, co-authored with Sally Osberg of the Skoll Foundation, is entitled *Getting Beyond Better: How Social Entrepreneurship Works* (2015). It helped them win the 2015 Thinkers50 Distinguished Achievement Award for Social Enterprise.

Martin is the former dean of the Rotman School of Management at the University of Toronto (where he now holds Premier's Chair in Productivity and Competitiveness).

Michael E. Porter

Regarded as the father of modern business strategy, Michael Porter is the outstanding business thinker of his generation. Porter's influence on business strategy has been immense. His Five Forces Framework is still taught in every business school in the world. Since the financial crisis of

2008, Porter's theory of Shared Value has led the way in a re-evaluation of the role and expectations of capitalism.

A renowned economist, Porter returned to the No. 1 place in the Thinkers50 in 2015 after previously topping the list in 2007. According to *Fortune* magazine, he has 'influenced more executives – and more nations – than any other business professor on earth.'

Porter's first book, *Competitive Strategy*, has defined the modern strategy field since its publication in 1980. Throughout his career at Harvard Business School, he has brought economic theory and strategy concepts to bear on many of the most challenging problems facing corporations, economies and societies, including market competition and company strategy, economic development, the environment, and health care.

Named a University Professor by Harvard University – the highest recognition that can be awarded to a Harvard faculty member – Porter and his competitive doctrine continue to spur catalytic change across global business, government and social sectors.

Since 2001, Porter has devoted considerable attention to competition in the health care system. And most recently, he has applied his ideas to show how smart, connected products (those containing embedded sensors, processors and software to create connectivity) are creating a technological revolution that will transform competition and have profound implications for society.

Porter's work remains as relevant as ever. His *Harvard Business Review* article, 'How Smart, Connected Products Are Transforming Competition' (November 2014), details a new era in competition driven by information technology and the Internet of Things.

He has also written about economic development and competitiveness, focusing on the micro-economic underpinnings of national and regional economic development. His book *The Competitive Advantage of Nations* (1990) was the initial foundation of this body of work. He also created the Cluster Mapping Project, which pioneered the rigorous measurement of economic geography.

Porter plays an active role in US economic policy with the Executive Branch and Congress, and has led national economic strategy programs in numerous countries. In environmental policy, Porter proposed the 'Porter Hypothesis' in the early 1990s, which put forward the novel theory that strict environmental standards were not in conflict with company profitability or national competitiveness, but could enhance both.

Porter also developed a body of work on the role of corporations in society. His ideas have changed the way companies approach philanthropy and corporate social responsibility, and he introduced the concept of creating shared value in a 2011 paper with Mark Kramer that shows how capitalism itself can be the best route to real solutions to many social problems.

He has also led the development of the conceptual framework underlying the new Social Progress Index. First released in 2014 and covering 132 countries, the Index rigorously measures each country's social progress across multiple dimensions to complement traditional measurement focused solely on economic performance and GDP per capita.

Only communicate #9

Imagine you are a CEO. You take your top team away for a strategy session at a suitably well-furnished hotel somewhere in the countryside. Over two days of discussions, you emerge with a great new strategy for the organization. The future is mapped out with brilliant simplicity, markets will be disrupted, the competition won't know what has hit them. You get back to the office and let some bright consultants loose to test out the strategy. The numbers add up, the insights into where the market is going appear robust, and then … . Well, and then you put the brilliantly conceived strategy into the top drawer of your desk (next to the hip flask, picture of your first love and ancient teddy bear).

Sound far-fetched? Of course, if you don't tell anyone about your strategy it is unlikely to become reality. How can you galvanize people if they don't actually know what the strategy is?

Yet, this is what happens repeatedly in organizations. The creation of strategy is something which business schools, consultants, coaches and advisors have mastered. In contrast, actually communicating the strategy to the world is something which tends to be left to minions or to forces of nature. CEOs don't put the strategy documents into a drawer and then forget about them, but sometimes they might as well have done.

In many organizations fundamental questions remain hanging in the air. What is a company's mission? And what is its strategy to win in the market? Basic questions, but ones which often go unanswered by some of the world's leading corporations.

Research by ECSI Consulting (ecsi-consulting.com) looked at the top 50 companies in the Fortune 500 ranking of US companies. It examined how the companies communicated their mission and strategies in their annual reports and websites.

The research found that vagueness, inconsistency and elusiveness are the reality – worrying news for any investors seeking to find out more about a company before investing or for potential employees of these corporate giants trying to learn more about the companies.

'The results are disturbing for investors, employees and many others,' says Alessandro Di Fiore of ECSI (who we featured on the Thinkers50 Radar for 2016). 'How can companies and their leaders be held to account if their purpose and the strategies they are seeking to execute are not clearly and consistently communicated?'

While 94 percent included their mission statement on their website, only half of the companies included their mission statement in their annual report.

Strategies are similarly difficult to pin down, i.e. a clear statement on how the company is going to win in the market and gain clients. A total of 58 percent of the companies included their strategy in their annual report. But a mere 12 percent included a dedicated, clearly articulated strategy section. On websites, 54 percent included some kind of strategy description.

Strangely perhaps, the most elusive sector is the high-tech world of computing, ICT and telecoms. Here companies appear unwilling to be bound by static guidelines or held hostage by public statements of strategy. Perhaps the logic is that the tech world is moving so quickly that any notion of strategy is likely to be proved worthless, so it's better to be opportunistically vague about your intent.

But it's not only the fact that information is notable by its absence. When companies do share details of their missions and strategies, the results are often underwhelming.

The obvious is often restated with buzzwords added to suggest industry know-how. Goals, such as 'creating competitive advantage' or 'being innovative', are routinely mistaken for strategy. And there is a repetitive focus on 'maximizing shareholder value', 'delivering profitable growth' and so on.

'A good strategy description should answer three fundamental questions,' says Alessandro Di Fiore. 'How are we going to win in the market? How we are different? And why is that difference relevant for our existing and potential customers?'

But vagueness rules in many annual reports. Strategy statements are usually unable to answer the question: 'How is the company going to win in the market and attract customers?' The insurance giant AIG, for example, states: 'Our strategy is focused on enhancing the value and competitive position of our insurance businesses and investing our capital where we can achieve attractive risk-adjusted returns, while maintaining strong levels of liquidity and capital.'

Others make elusiveness their strategy. Apple is notably reticent while Walgreens, the drugstore chain, chooses to brazen it out with the simple statement: 'We do not provide detailed information on specific topics, such as our corporate strategy.'

Some companies do meet the strategic clarity challenge. 'Our strategy is to provide our members with a broad range of high quality merchandise at prices consistently lower than they can obtain elsewhere,' says Costco while Microsoft says its strategy is to 'build best-in-class platforms and productivity services for a mobile-first, cloud-first world'.

Says Alessandro Di Fiore:

> A strategy should be able to be distilled down to 15 compelling, meaningful and memorable words articulating how we are going to win in the marketplace. It needs then to be communicated clearly and consistently inside and outside. This research suggests there is still a long way to go for this to be achieved. Even on the most fundamental company's document for all stakeholders – the Annual Report – there are gaps.

You might say that annual reports and website information is for the external world and that companies may well be communicating their strategies brilliantly internally. This may be so in some organizations, but it seems unlikely. Vagueness and obfuscation are habitual and cultural. Where would you like to work? Where would you choose to invest your money? In a company which clearly and repeatedly articulates its mission and strategy or one which does not?

There is little doubt that communication issues are set to become ever more important as information becomes ever more pervasive and instantly communicated. There is no place to hide.

Talking with Columbia Business School's Rita McGrath, this is what she observed:

> The difference in leadership behavior that you're going to be seeing is an emphasis much more on information travelling fast. So I use the example of Ford and Alan Mulally, CEO at Ford, who basically said, you can't manage a secret. So we're going to see a lot less of the management of, bring me the numbers, hit the goals, don't bring me bad news, don't bring me a problem that you don't have a solution to. That kind of management, which works really well when things are stable, we're going to see that going away.
>
> We're going to see a lot more leadership that involves influencing people and getting people engaged. We're going to see much more candour, much more emphasis on being realistic and also much more emphasis on keeping individuals and networks engaged, because in the past you used to be able to say a hierarchical reward was going to be the thing, so you start off at level 14 and you end up at level two and that's Nirvana. And I think we will see much less of that in how we manage careers in the future or how leaders engage people in the future.

The twenty-first century is a time of transparent, instant communication – and that applies to your organization's strategy.

Strategic confusion #10

One of the most straight talking thinkers about strategy is the American academic Richard Rumelt. According to Rumelt, badly construed strategy has four hallmarks which should set alarm bells ringing. These are:

- Failure to face the problem: usually when the problem has not been properly defined.
- Mistaking goals for strategy: this was the mistake made by Lehman Brothers.
- Bad strategic objectives: beware a long list of objectives, which are not prioritized or even connected to each other.
- The final hallmark is what Rumelt calls 'fluff' – or hubris. Distrust a strategy that restates the obvious with buzzwords. Rumelt gives the example of a retail bank, which proclaimed: 'Our fundamental strategy is one of customer-centric intermediation.' In reality, intermediation is banking. Customer-centric was meaningless. So once the buzzwords were removed the bank's strategy boiled down to being a bank – tautological at best.

As Richard Rumelt has lamented, bad strategies are commonplace. And, in an era of constant and unpredictable change, the practical usefulness of strategy is increasingly – and loudly – questioned. The skeptics argue that it is all well and good to come up with a brilliantly formulated strategy, but quite another to implement it. By the time implementation begins, the business environment is liable to have changed and be in the process of changing even further.

During the early 1990s, the death knell for traditional approaches to strategy was sounded. 'The humane thing to do with most strategic planning processes is to kill them off,' concluded a report by OC&C Strategy Consultants.

'As "strategy" has blossomed, the competitiveness of Western companies has withered. This may be coincidence, but we think not,' noted C.K. Prahalad and Gary Hamel.

Research by the American Planning Forum found that a mere 25 percent of companies considered their planning processes to be effective. Similarly, in his book *The Rise and Fall of Strategic Planning*, Henry Mintzberg took on the full might of conventional planning orthodoxy. 'Too much analysis gets in our way. The failure of strategic planning is the failure of formalization,' said Mintzberg, identifying formalization as the fatal flaw of modern management.

Mintzberg argued the case for, what he labeled, strategic programing. His view was that strategy has for too long been housed in ivory towers built from corporate data and analysis. It had become distant from reality, when to have any viable commercial life strategy needs to become completely immersed in reality.

'Strategies appear at predetermined times, popping out when expected, full blown, all ready for implementation. It is almost as if they are immaculately conceived,' he caustically observed.

After a decent period of mourning, strategic planning began undergoing something of a rebirth. First, rather than being regarded as an annual ritual, strategy is now more commonly seen as a continuous process, a dialogue rather than a monologue. Second, the focus is on the big picture rather than on operational plans. Instead of weighty planning departments filled with bright minds producing great plans never to see the light of day, the emphasis is on strategy as part of corporate development with small teams working on distinct projects calling on outside consultants when necessary. The role of the consultants principally lies in benchmarking corporate performance, monitoring and identifying external trends and helping develop a corporate vision.

All this confirms that, amid the constant rising and falling, strategy remains deeply bedded in confusion. Rarely has so much theorizing amounted to so little effective practice. The confusion over such a well-debated issue can be attributed to a number of factors.

Confusion over what strategy actually is. There is a confusion between what an organization is actually doing, what it says it is doing and what it should be doing. In practice, strategy tends to embrace all three.

The sheer profusion of approaches. In the faddish world of management thinking no single subject has generated so many bright ideas – from strategic intent to core competencies, blue oceans to balanced scorecards.

Confusion with the actual processes of developing and then implementing strategy. The process remains clouded by verbiage. Does an organization study its marketplace and competitive environment and then change itself to meet perceived opportunities? Indeed, Michael Porter defines strategy as the positioning of the company relative to its industry environment. Or, does strategy begin with the organization, examining what it excels at and then aim to make the most of those assets in the current environment?

The shift from linear thinking to emergent chaos. In the current business environment where the calls for change and transformation are constant, the traditional methods of formulating and implementing strategy are increasingly questioned. The conventional approach takes as its guiding light the acronym MOST (Mission, Objectives, Strategy and Tactics). This offers an orderly progression from creating a mission to making the strategy happen.

Life is no longer so simple. Says Andrew Campbell of the Ashridge Strategic Management Centre:

> In practice, the real process of strategy development and direction setting is much more messy, experimental, uncertain, iterative and driven from the bottom upwards. There are five reasons for

> rejecting the MOST framework. First, the competitive economic system in which companies act provides constraints that are often interpreted as objectives. Second, strategy and objectives are intertwined, not linear. Third, it is useless to develop a separation between strategy, tactics and operations – insights about creating value come as often from operating details as from broad strategic concepts. Fourth, academics and consultants differ in their views about how insights can best be developed and captured. Fifth, there are also differences in view about how best to implement strategy in an uncertain world.

The battle between analysis and intuition. From this it would seem that the days of highly analytical, rational, strategy creation are past. But, strategy can neither be purely rational nor purely intuitive. Indeed, one of the core skills of managers is to know when and how to use their intuitive judgement of a particular situation.

Confusion is endemic. But, argues London Business School's Costas Markides, it need not be:

> The confusion surrounding strategy manifests itself in a variety of ways. But, in reality, the confusion is unfortunate – and unjustified. Strategy is a very simple thing – at its simplest it is five or six creative ideas that tell us how our company is to fight the competitive battle in its industry. It is not a plan; it is not a hundred-page report; it is not a budget; and it is not a goal. It is just five or six creative ideas. If your company cannot put down its strategy on one sheet of paper then it does not have a strategy.

The problem is that managers have been reared on an unhealthy diet of weighty reports and pithy distillation remains an elusive art.

Resources

Richard Rumelt, *Good Strategy Bad Strategy*, Profile, 2012.

Military inspiration #11

Soldiers have a surprisingly lengthy heritage as managerial exemplars – both in terms of practice and theory. Look back to Hadrian, the enigmatic wall-building Roman Emperor from 117 to 138. He was a champion of people power long before the advent of such niceties as human resource departments. Pomp and circumstance were not for him. His military reputation was forged on his willingness to share the same conditions as his troops. One anecdote describes his refusal to wear his cloak or cap no matter what the weather. Similarly, Hadrian was reputed to join his troops on lengthy marches in full armor.

A series of humanitarian decisions cemented his reputation. He prohibited castration, and was concerned about slaves. Hadrian was also a globetrotter. He didn't seek to control his empire from Rome but traveled throughout it. In modern parlance, he accepted the diversity of his empire – coins issued during his reign celebrated the numerous provinces he had visited. Hadrian also brought to an end the inexorable Roman expansionism. He sought to draw a line around the empire rather than engaging in endless foreign wars. (Perhaps he realized that most corporations go bust in the midst of expanding.)

Hadrian was also reputed to have had an eye for financial management – though he started his reign by announcing an amnesty of all debts owed to the government. While his predecessor frittered away the money in the treasury, Hadrian was more frugal and built up reserves to fund building projects and social welfare programs. At the same time, he didn't raise taxes. (Modern politicians would no doubt like to know exactly how he managed to achieve the political equivalent of squaring the circle.)

Claiming similar credence as a path-breaking managerial practitioner was the Duke of Wellington (1769–1851). Wellington can lay claim to managing by wandering around during the Napoleonic Wars. Historian John Keegan has noted:

> [Wellington's methods] required a particularly intense 'managerial' style – 'taking trouble' with the battle, as Wellington himself would later put it. The general must make himself the eyes of his own army … must constantly change position to deal with crises as they occur along the front of his sheltered line, must remain at the point of crises until it is resolved and must still keep alert to anticipate the development of crises elsewhere.

We digress, but the point remains that strategy and the military are inextricably linked. Indeed, the book which ignited the business world's interest in strategy has military inspirations. In 1954 Alfred Chandler (himself formerly of the US Navy) was invited to create and teach a course at the Naval War College in Newport, Rhode Island on 'the basis of national strategy'.

Chandler later recalled:

> William Rietzal, who was at the College in another capacity, had become interested in the post-second world war changes in military organizational structures, particularly those that came with the creation of the post-war Department of Defense. I was then developing my interest in the evolution of modern business structures. So we agreed that each of us would write a book on our respective intellectual concerns. Rietzal never completed his book. Mine came out in 1962.

The book was *Strategy and Structure*.

From his research into major US corporations between 1850 and 1920, Chandler argues that a firm's structure is dictated by its chosen strategy – 'Unless structure follows strategy, inefficiency results'. First, a company should establish a strategy and then seek to create the structure appropriate to achieving it. Chandler defines strategy as 'the determination of the long-term goals and objectives of an enterprise, and the adoption of courses of action and the allocation of resources necessary for carrying out these goals.'

> Our view of strategy has changed from the classic Coca-Cola vs. Pepsi market-share fight to how do you shape the emergence of the new opportunity areas, whether it's branchless banking, satellite telephony, or genetic engineering.
>
> **Gary Hamel**

Chandler observes that organizational structures in companies such as Du Pont, Sears Roebuck, General Motors and Standard Oil were driven by the changing demands and pressures of the marketplace. He traces the market-driven proliferation of product lines in Du Pont and General Motors and concludes that this proliferation led to a shift from a functional, monolithic organizational form to a more loosely-coupled divisional structure. (Interestingly, Chandler's family had historical connections with DuPont – and DuPont was also Chandler's middle name. At the time DuPont also controlled General Motors.)

Said Chandler:

> The management structures whose evolution are described in *Strategy and Structure* were primarily adopted by enterprises in increasingly capital and knowledge intensive industries, as pointed out in its concluding chapter. This is because the new multidivisional structure permitted the commercializing of new technologies producing products for different markets. For example, chemical companies were from the 1920s on producing a variety of chemicals, fibres, film, finishes, plastics, explosives and other things. The structure thus permitted them to lower their unit costs through the economies of scope as well as scale.

Until recent times, Chandler's conclusion that structure follows strategy has largely been accepted as a fact of corporate life. The debate was then rekindled. 'I think he got it exactly wrong,' says Tom Peters with typical forthrightness. 'For it is the structure of the organization that determines, over time, the choices that it makes about the markets in attacks.'

Another contrary view comes from Kathleen M. Eisenhardt of Stanford:

> The Chandler idea that strategy is set and then structure follows makes sense in clear, static markets. In ambiguous, dynamic markets, the two are much more intertwined. In my view, in the overall approach, structure and, more important, the processes by which structure changes are the constants while strategy changes.

Counters Gary Hamel:

> Those who dispute Chandler's thesis that structure follows strategy miss the point. Of course strategy and structure are inextricably intertwined. Chandler's point was that new challenges give rise to new structures. The challenges of size and complexity, coupled with advances in communications and techniques of management control produced divisionalization and decentralization. These same forces, several generations on, are now driving us towards new structural solutions – the 'federated organization', the multi-company coalition, and the virtual company. Few historians are prescient. Chandler was.

While this debate rumbles on, Chandler's place in the canon of strategy literature remains secure. In particular, he was highly influential in the trend among large organizations for decentralization in the 1960s and 1970s. While in 1950 around 20 percent of Fortune 500 corporations were decentralized; this had increased to 80 percent by 1970. In *Strategy and Structure*, Chandler praises Alfred Sloan's decentralization of General Motors in the 1920s. He was later influential in the transformation of AT&T in the 1980s from what was in effect a production-based bureaucracy to a marketing organization.

The book also ignited the strategy-based consulting industry. Prior to the 1960s, McKinsey was not a strategy firm, since strategy as a discipline did not exist, but instead concentrated on restructuring organizations. Similarly, BCG, which was founded in the early 1960s after Bruce Henderson left Arthur D. Little, also benefited from this new interest in strategy as a subject.

Strategy and Structure also contributed to the 'professionalization of management'. Chandler traces the historical development of what he labels 'the managerial revolution' fueled by the rise of oil-based energy, the development of the steel, chemical and engineering industries and a dramatic rise in the scale of production and the size of companies. Increases in scale, Chandler observes, led to business owners having to recruit a new breed of professional manager.

Chandler believed that the roles of the salaried manager and technician are vital, and talks of the 'visible hand' of management coordinating the flow of product to customers more efficiently than Adam Smith's 'invisible hand' of the market (see Chandler's 1977 book, *The Visible Hand*). The logical progression from this is that organizations and their managements require a planned economy rather than a capitalist free-for-all dominated by the unpredictable whims of market forces. In the more sedate times in which *Strategy and Structure* was written, the lure of the visible hand proved highly persuasive.

Resources

Interview with Alfred Chandler by Jorge Nascimento Rodrigues, 2002.
Tom Peters, *Liberation Management*, Alfred A. Knopf, 1992.
John Keegan, *The Mask of Command*, Penguin Books, 1987.

What strategy looks like #12

Strategy is a little like art. People tend to recognize great strategy when they see it. This is usually in the neatness of retrospect.

Take the case of Thomas Watson Jr. deciding to commit IBM to the development of a new line of computers in 1962. He bet the company on the future: a big company and, as it turned out, a big future. The S/360s revolutionized the industry.

Over recent years the reign of Thomas Watson Jr. (1914–93) at IBM has had a bad press. To some he is the son who inherited control of a corporate juggernaut and did little to put his own stamp on its destination. To others he is the man who brought IBM into the technological era and who mapped out how values and culture could shape an entire organization. In 1987 Watson was hailed by *Fortune* as 'the most successful capitalist in history'.

Whichever interpretation is correct, Watson had a significant role in the shaping of the modern IBM – a company whose trials and tribulations continue to fill the media. Watson Junior became chief executive in 1956 and retired in 1970. He was then US ambassador in Moscow until 1980.

Watson propelled IBM to the forefront of the technological and corporate revolution of the sixties and seventies. Most notably, Watson invested heavily in the development of System/360 which formed the basis of the company's success in the 1970s and 1980s. More money – $5 billion – was spent on developing the 360 than on the development of the nuclear bomb.

> The real challenge in crafting strategy lies in detecting the subtle discontinuities that may undermine a business in the future. And for that there is no technique, no programme, just a sharp mind in touch with the situation.
>
> **Henry Mintzberg**

While the decision to go ahead with the 360 was brave and significant, Watson can also lay claim to another important decision: his decision to codify the IBM culture. Under Watson, the corporate culture and the company's values became all-important. They were the glue that kept a sprawling international operation under control. Watson created a blueprint for the modern corporation circa 1960.

The three basic beliefs on which IBM was built were: give full consideration to the individual employee; spend a lot of time making customers happy; and go the last mile to do things right. These had been established under Watson Sr., a man who knew all about customer service long before it was taken up by the gurus. But, while Watson Sr. was content to drum the message home, his son took it a step further.

Watson Jr. codified and clarified what IBM stood for – most notably in his book, *A Business and Its Beliefs* (1963). Central to this were the company's central beliefs (or what would now be called core values).

Whether IBM hit trouble because it failed to change or adapt its beliefs to new times is difficult to determine. Watson saw it coming. 'I'm worried that IBM could become a big, inflexible organization which won't be able to change when the computer business goes through its next shift,' Watson told Chris Argyris of Harvard in the 1950s when Argyris did some work for the company. Watson saw the future but couldn't mobilize the corporate culture he did so much to clarify in structures or practices which enabled IBM to pick up the baton.

So, what does the IBM story tell us about strategy?

First, it is open to interpretation. No strategy is neat and tidy in planning and execution. Strategy is a messy business.

Second, greatness often equates with boldness. Even giants need to bet the company sometimes. The bets just get bigger.

Third, it is often easier to execute strategy efficiently when you have solid foundations. IBM had just that in its culture and values. Culture is – or can be – a source of competitive advantage. Watson said that a culture could only be sustained by 'a sound set of beliefs, on which it premises all its policies and actions. Next, I believe that the most important single factor in corporate success is faithful adherence to those beliefs … beliefs must always come before policies, practices, and goals. The latter must always be altered if they are seen to violate fundamental beliefs.'

Beliefs never change. Change everything else, but never the basic truths on which the company is based – 'If an organization is to meet the challenges of a changing world, it must be prepared to change everything about itself except beliefs as it moves through corporate life … The only sacred cow in an organization should be its basic philosophy of doing business.' In a world dominated by pursuit of cash cows, this particular bovine truism is often forgotten.

Resources

Thomas Watson, *A Business and Its Beliefs*, McGraw Hill, 2003.

The mind of the strategist #13

Kenichi Ohmae is an impressive man. Visiting his office in downtown Tokyo is to step into a parallel universe of influence and connectivity. The building is also home for Ohmae, not to mention the slightly bewildering variety of businesses he is active in (a business school and broadcasting company among others). There is a concert hall in the building as well. Ohmae is, after all, a gifted flautist, not to mention a nuclear physicist, a prodigious author with dozens of books to his credit, politician and long-time star of the consulting firm, McKinsey and Company. Indeed, when he left McKinsey to stand for the governorship of Tokyo in 1995, the consultancy firm's departure announcement noted Ohmae was 'a great consultant, a compelling speaker, an incredibly prolific writer, a musician and a motorcyclist'. As career epitaphs go this is one most people would accept!

Among all his other books – and there are many not yet available in English – the one which stands out for its influence is *The Mind of the Strategist*. The book was published in Japan in 1975, but did not reach the American market until 1982.

The subtitle of the first edition was 'The art of Japanese business' and the book was published in the West at the height of enthusiasm for and interest in Japanese management methods – when the book was first published in Japan, the West remained studiously uninterested in the possibility of learning from Japanese best practice.

In *The Mind of the Strategist* Ohmae challenges the simplistic, but then widely held belief, that Japanese management was a matter of company songs and lifetime employment. Instead, Ohmae argues that Japanese success could be significantly attributed to the nature of Japanese strategic thinking. This, says Ohmae, is 'basically creative and intuitive and rational' – though none of these characteristics were evident in the usual Western stereotype of Japanese management. Offering solace to the bemused and increasingly uncompetitive West, Ohmae suggests that the necessary creativity can be learned.

Ohmae points out that unlike large US corporations, Japanese businesses tend not to have large strategic planning staffs. Instead they often have a single, naturally talented strategist with 'an idiosyncratic mode of thinking in which company, customers, and competition merge in a dynamic interaction out of which a comprehensive set of objectives and plans for action eventually crystallizes'.

Ohmae explains that an effective business strategy is one by which a company can gain significant ground on its competitors at an acceptable cost to itself. This can be achieved in four ways: by focusing on the key factors for success, by building on relative superiority, through pursuing aggressive initiatives, and through utilizing strategic degrees of freedom – focusing on innovation in areas, which are untouched by competitors. While the outcome or objective is the same from East to West, Japanese entrepreneurs use an holistic and intuitive approach at the beginning, as opposed to the statistics and surveys often used in large Western corporations.

> The job of the strategist is to achieve superior performance, relative to competition, in the key factors for success of the business.
>
> **Kenichi Ohmae**

The central thrust of the book is that strategy as epitomized by the Japanese approach is irrational and non-linear. (Previously, the Japanese had been feted in the West for the brilliance of their rationality and the far-sighted remorselessness of their thinking.)

'In strategic thinking, one first seeks a clear understanding of the particular character of each element of a situation and then makes the fullest possible use of human brain power to restructure the elements in the most advantageous way,' writes Ohmae.

The Mind of the Strategist is not an unquestioning eulogy to the Japanese approach to strategy. Indeed, Ohmae notes the decline in naturally strategic thinkers in both Japan and the West. Both systems, he says, encourage orthodoxy to the extent that innovative strategic thinking is neither encouraged nor possible.

The Mind of the Strategist began the process of questioning the then pervasive Japanese mythology through providing interpretations of strategy which were not hidebound by habitual cultural or traditional behavior. It opened minds, a task Kenichi Ohmae is especially suited to.

Resources

Kenichi Ohmae, *The Mind of the Strategist*, McGraw Hill, 1991.

Strategy, seriously #14

In the early 1960s while the world discovered love, hallucinogenics and Jimi Hendrix, managers discovered strategy as their new holy grail. They did so, not in San Francisco or at Woodstock, but in Igor Ansoff's *Corporate Strategy*, published in 1965. 'This book represented a kind of crescendo in the development of strategic planning theory, offering a degree of elaboration seldom attempted since,' Henry Mintzberg later observed.

Unstintingly serious, analytical and complex, *Corporate Strategy*, had a highly significant impact on the business world. It propelled consideration of strategy into a new dimension. Ansoff said:

> Strategic management is a comprehensive procedure which starts with a strategic diagnosis and guides a firm through a series of additional steps which culminate in new products, markets and technologies, as well as new capabilities. The end product of strategic decisions is deceptively simple; a combination of products and markets is selected for the firm. This combination is arrived at by addition of new product-markets, divestment from some old ones, and expansion of the present position.

While the end product was simple, the processes and decisions beforehand produced a labyrinth followed only by the most dedicated of managers. Ansoff's subtitle was 'An Analytical Approach to Business Policy for Growth and Expansion'. The book provided a highly complex 'cascade of decisions'. Analysis – and in particular gap analysis (the gap between where you are now and where you want to be) – was the key to unlocking strategy.

The book also brought the concept of synergy to a wide audience for the first time. Today, the word is overused and much abused. In Ansoff's original creation it was simply summed up as 'the 2+2=5' effect. In his later books, Ansoff refined his definition of synergy to any 'effect which can produce a combined return on the firm's resources greater than the sum of its parts'.

One of us (Stuart) interviewed Ansoff in the late 1980s. He recounted his colorful start in life – born in Vladivostock to a Russian mother in 1918 – and how the search for inspiration had included a case of whisky and seclusion. By then Ansoff was fighting an intellectual rearguard action.

While *Corporate Strategy* was a notable book for its time, it produced what Ansoff himself labeled 'paralysis by analysis': repeatedly making strategic plans which remained unimplemented. He wrote:

> Strategic planning was a plausible invention, and received an enthusiastic reception from the business community. But subsequent experience with strategic planning led to mixed results. In a minority of firms, strategic planning restored their profitability and became an established part of the management process. However a substantial majority encountered a phenomenon, which was named 'paralysis by analysis': strategic plans were made but remained unimplemented, and profits/growth continued to stagnate.

Undaunted, Ansoff looked again at his entire theory. His logic was impressively simple – either strategic planning was a bad idea, or it was part of a broader concept which was not fully developed and needed to be enhanced in order to make strategic planning effective. Characteristically, he sought the answer in extensive research. He examined acquisitions by American companies between 1948 and 1968 and concluded that acquisitions which were based on an articulated strategy fared considerably better than those which were opportunistic decisions.

Reinforced by his conviction that strategy was a valid, if incomplete, concept, Ansoff followed up *Corporate Strategy* with *Strategic Management* (1979) and *Implanting Strategic Management* (1984). In each of these he sought a broader concept which would include strategic planning and would assure effective implementation of strategic plans.

Using the concept of strategic management, Ansoff formulated a Strategic Success Paradigm which specifies conditions which optimize a firm's profitability. This paradigm (the result of 'fifteen years of sweat, tears and smiles and occasional flashes of creativity') has five key elements:

1. There is no universal success formula for all firms.
2. The driving variable which dictates the strategy required for success of a firm is the level of turbulence in its environment.
3. A firm's success cannot be optimized unless the aggressiveness of its strategy is aligned with the turbulence in its environment.
4. A firm's success cannot be optimized unless management capability is also aligned with the environment.
5. The key internal capability variables which jointly determine a firm's success, are: cognitive, psychological, sociological, political and anthropological.

> Those oft are strategems which errors seem,
> Nor is it Homer nods, but we that dream.
>
> **Alexander Pope, poet**

Being aware of the patchy record of strategic planning, Ansoff (with the assistance of his graduate students) devoted the next eleven years to empirical validation of the Success Paradigm. The paradigm was tested in over 500 firms in the US, Japan, Indonesia, Algeria, Abu Dabhi, Australia and Ethiopia. The statistical results gave strong support to the paradigm. Ansoff translated the paradigm into a diagnostic instrument, called 'Strategic Readiness Diagnosis' and used it in his consulting practice.

Today, Ansoff's part in the development of strategy is somewhat neglected. Given that we live in the era of Big Data it is ironic that a man who did so much to champion serious analysis is overlooked.

Resources

Igor Ansoff's books don't make for light reading, but they were hugely influential. They include *Corporate Strategy*, McGraw Hill, 1965; *Strategic Management*, Macmillan, 1979); and *Implanting Strategic Management* (2nd edn), Prentice Hall, 1990.

The context just got bigger #15

In 1995, the *Californian Management Review* published an article, 'Integrated Strategy: Market and Non-market Components', by economist and Stanford University professor David P. Baron. It argued that effective strategic management must encompass both market and non-market strategy.

The logic was compelling then – and is even more so now. There is a substantial non-market component to any business environment. Non-market means any activity that is not based on or directly driven by market forces. The non-market space provides the social and political context in which all businesses have to operate. There is and has always been a nuanced negotiation between the two spheres that legitimizes and defines any firm's licence to operate. The patterns and actions that take place in the non-market sphere affect an organization's ability to create value by increasing its overall performance.

Baron defines the non-market environment as including, 'those interactions that are intermediated by the public, stakeholders, government, the media, and public institutions'. This is a very different environment to the market where interactions tend to be voluntary and involve economic transactions intermediated by markets or private agreements.

In the non-market space, notes Baron, characteristics such as majority rule, due process, broad enfranchisement and collective action, are important. Interactions may be voluntary, like a firm lobbying government departments, but are often involuntary such as government legislation and regulations, and product and service boycotts by pressure groups.

In Baron's view, four 'I's characterize the non-market environment. Issues – which are what non-market strategies address, revising legislation, for example. Institutions such as the governments, government departments and regulatory bodies deal with non-market issues. Interests are individuals and groups involved in issues. Regulation of energy markets, for example, would involve energy companies, activist groups, consumers, manufacturers and suppliers, and the media, among others. While information is what the interested parties know that is relevant to the non-market issue.

> Strategy is, above all else, the search for above-average returns.
>
> **Gary Hamel**

One of the difficulties with non-market strategy lies with its definition. Says Warwick Business School's Kamel Mellahi:

> Any concept that is defined in terms of what it is not – i.e. non-market – is problematic. But alternative descriptions – such as CSR (corporate social responsibility) or lobbying – fail to capture its full scope. Alternative terms have also failed to catch on. Perhaps it should be called 'social and political strategy'?

Yale School of Management's David Bach emphasizes the fact that non-market strategy is a holistic process, requiring a firm's management to simultaneously monitor its positioning among stakeholders – including the arena of public opinion.

'Few firms are prepared to do the hard work and commit long-term to developing an effective non-market strategy. Fewer still understand how to integrate market and non-market strategies to sustain competitive advantage,' says Bach before venturing an answer to the question of what is non-market strategy and why is it important now?

> Non-market strategy is simply the idea that the business environment consists of more than just markets. There are the other

> stakeholders who bear directly on a company's ability to create and defend competitive advantage: governments, regulators, non-governmental organizations, the media and so forth. We can call these 'non-market actors' and they become increasingly important in terms of the influence that they have on the company.

Just as a firm strategically manages its market environment and comes up with a plan for creating competitive advantage, it should do the same for the non-market environment.

According to Bach and his co-author David Allen:

> Non-market strategy starts with a simple, dual premise – first, that issues and actors 'beyond the market' increasingly affect the bottom line, and, second, that they can be managed just as strategically as conventional 'core business' activities within markets. The challenge for CEOs and their leadership teams is one of simultaneous separation and integration. To successfully manage beyond the market, executives must recognize the important differences between the firm's market and non-market environments but then take an integrated, coherent and strategic approach to both arenas. This is the key to turning perceived 'non-business' issues into strategic opportunities and thereby building sustainable competitive advantage.

In their work Bach and Allen discuss a number of facets of non-market strategy. They address the role of globalization as a catalyst for non-market strategy development, for example. There are, say Bach and Allen, four factors linked to globalization that are driving non-market strategy. The first is that globalization means companies have to address multiple audiences across continents and countries, and thus navigate many non-market environments, that often reflect markedly different social and political values.

Second, as Bach and Allen point out, it is not just business that is becoming global, but also the influence of NGOs and activists. Using social media and other modern communications technologies, activists can respond quickly, reporting events wherever they occur within hours, and bringing them to the attention of consumers around the world.

Third, doing business across the globe means more market opportunities, but it also means being exposed to many regulatory environments, regional, national, and international. Governments have created many more regulatory agencies. Regulatory frameworks are far from uniform.

The last factor is that greater globalization has also led to increased market competition. When organizations have routinely used outsourcing to lower costs and fragmented their value chains across the world, finding a competitive edge proves ever more difficult. Understandably, organizations are looking beyond market strategy to non-market strategy to capture that competitive advantage. The arena of strategy has never been bigger.

Resources

David Allen and David Bach, 'What every CEO needs to understand about non-market strategy', *Sloan Management Review*, Spring 2010.

How Nelson did it #16

One of the most interesting commentators on strategy is Richard Rumelt, author of *Good Strategy/Bad Strategy* (2011). The book opens with a brief account of Admiral Horatio Nelson's naval victory at the Battle of Trafalgar in 1805, when the British fleet, consisting of 27 ships, defeated the combined forces of the French and Spanish, which numbered 33 ships. Nelson won the day by adopting an unconventional strategy. Flouting the naval convention of the time, he divided his smaller fleet into two columns and sailed them perpendicularly into the enemy fleet to cut the Franco-Spanish line.

Nelson knew that his lead ships would be vulnerable to Franco-Spanish guns until they could close on the opposing fleet. He gambled that the less well-trained enemy gunners would not be able to capitalize on their advantage. He was proved right. The French and Spanish cannons were not able to compensate for the heavy swell and missed their opportunity to sink the British ships while they could not return fire. Once the battle was joined, the superiority of the British seamanship was decisive. The French and Spanish lost 22 ships. The British lost none. This, as Rumelt points out, is an example of a good strategy:

> Nelson's challenge was that he was outnumbered. His strategy was to risk his lead ships in order to break the coherence of his enemy's fleet. With coherence lost, he judged, the more experienced English captains would come out on top in the ensuing melee. Good strategy almost always looks this simple and obvious and does not take a thick deck of PowerPoint slides to explain. It does not pop

> out of some 'strategic management' tool, matrix, chart, triangle or fill-in-the-blanks scheme. Instead, a talented leader identifies the one or two critical issues in the situation – the pivot points that can multiply the effectiveness of effort – and then focuses and concentrates action and resources on them.

Rumelt provides a timely reminder that strategy is all about matching the resources at your disposal to a specific situation or context and using them in unexpected ways to create an advantage or overcome a disadvantage. Usually, that involves using strengths against weaknesses. But a good strategy also has a coherence of design that minimizes risks and maximizes the chances of success. In short, a good strategy is a joined-up strategy. Leaders must appraise the situation facing the organization and find a way to overcome the obstacles to reach objectives. Sometimes that requires it to take a risk. But it should always be a calculated risk – and one that is taken without leaving the organization unnecessarily exposed or vulnerable.

As Rumelt explains:

> A leader's most important responsibility is identifying the biggest challenges to forward progress and devising a coherent approach to overcoming them. In contexts ranging from corporate direction to national security, strategy matters. Yet we have become so accustomed to strategy as exhortation that we hardly blink an eye when a leader spouts slogans and announces high-sounding goals, calling the mixture a 'strategy'.

He contrasts Nelson's high-risk strategy with that of Lehman Brothers. By 2006, the US property market had peaked. A rise in the Fed's interest rates led to an increase in foreclosures. Lehman's CEO Richard Fuld's strategic response was to continue to gain market share by growing faster than its competitors. To do so Lehman would increase its 'risk appetite' as Wall Street parlance put it. It would take on the deals that other banks were rejecting. Unfortunately, this was not a rounded strategy – it lacked a response to the problems of taking on greater risk. Without this it was little more than blind ambition – and a very bad strategy indeed.

Rumelt observes:

> Operating with only 3 percent equity, and much of its debt supplied on a very short-term basis, this policy should have been accompanied by clever ways of mitigating the increased risk. A good strategy recognizes the nature of the challenge and offers a way of surmounting it. Simply being ambitious is not a strategy. In 2008, Lehman Brothers ended its 158 years as an investment bank with a crash that sent the global financial system into a tailspin. Here, the consequences of bad strategy were disastrous for Lehman, the United States and the world.

In strategic thinking, one first seeks a clear understanding of the particular character of each element of a situation and then makes the fullest possible use of human brain power to restructure the elements in the most advantageous way.

Kenichi Ohmae, flautist, nuclear physicist, consultant, author and politician

Rumelt's work offers a cautionary tale for all strategists. There are two dimensions, he says, to a good strategy:

> Having a coherent strategy — one that coordinates policies and actions. A good strategy doesn't just draw on existing strength; it creates strength through the coherence of its design. Most organizations of any size don't do this. Rather, they pursue multiple objectives that are unconnected with one another or, worse, that conflict with one another.
>
> The creation of new strengths through subtle shifts in viewpoint. An insightful reframing of a competitive situation can create whole new patterns of advantage and weakness. The most powerful strategies arise from such game-changing insights.

Resources

Richard Rumelt, *Good Strategy Bad Strategy*, Profile, 2012.

The analytical stranglehold #17

The fuel for the modern growth in interest in all things strategic has been analysis. While analysis has been the watchword, data has been the password. Managers have assumed that anything which could not be analyzed could not be managed. The last forty years have seen a ceaseless quest for things, actions and decisions which can be analyzed. The belief in analysis is part of a search for a logical commercial regime, a system of management which will, under any circumstances, produce a successful result. But, effective analysis does not guarantee effective, or even appropriate, implementation.

Indeed, all the analysis in the world can lead to decisions which are plainly wrong. Kodak had all the data about its markets, yet reached the wrong conclusions. It is a problem not restricted to business. British Prime Minister Harold Macmillan was once asked what was the most difficult thing about his job. 'Events, my dear boy, events,' he replied. For all its usefulness, analysis does not dictate events. Big data does not automatically equate to big insights and solutions. Things may add up, but they don't necessarily work.

'Strategy-making is an immensely complex process involving the most sophisticated, subtle and at times subconscious of human cognitive and social processes,' writes Henry Mintzberg. 'While hard data may inform the intellect, it is largely soft data that generates wisdom. They may be difficult to "analyze", but they are indispensable for synthesis – the key to strategy making.' As Mintzberg puts it: 'Real strategists need to get their hands dirty digging for ideas.'

Roger Martin, former dean of the Rotman School of Management at the University of Toronto, is known for his work on integrative thinking as a means of solving complex problems and has argued that organizations should adopt a more design-based approach to thinking. Designers get close to the end-user and use abductive reasoning – pragmatic guesswork – to create more value. They balance two kinds of models of value creation – analytical thinking and intuitive thinking – to produce 'design thinking'. The mix is the thing.

Says Alessandro Di Fiore of the consulting firm ECSI:

> Sound qualitative judgment is behind most market-beating innovations. Building a qualitative judgment capability requires a significant shift for most companies, which are deeply ingrained in number-driven innovation. The pathway should reflect the starting point. The first step should be an assessment of the company's current capability. Then, companies should agree on its critical axes of change which might reflect some of or all six presented rules.
>
> Finally, they should agree on an appropriate ambition level and develop a shared road map to attain it. For many companies, to develop such a capability will remain a source of frustration. For the best ones, however, it will represent an exciting journey. Figuring out how to harness the power of qualitative judgement as a driver of innovation and growth could represent the ultimate competitive advantage in today's knowledge society.

Di Fiore is right. There are two basic problems with the reliance on analysis. First, it is all technique. Watching the implementation of a strategy which is solely based on analysis is like listening to a synthesizer recreate the sound of a Stradivarius. It is hollow and de-humanized. Even in the technological age, de-humanized management remains a contradiction in terms.

The second problem is more fundamental. Analysis produces a self-increasing loop. The belief is that more and more analysis will bring safer and safer decisions. If analysis is insufficient, the manager begins to feel guilty. How can they produce a strategy when the data is non-existent or insubstantial? To assuage the guilt they carry out some more analysis. The process continues, relentlessly delaying any decision-making. In such cases, strategy is driven by guilt and fueled by analysis. Eventually, enough data is bound to filter through and a strategy of sorts will emerge. The process is, however, time-consuming and tortuous. Before the resulting strategy becomes action it is likely that the self-perpetuating combination of analysis and guilt will continue to interfere with and slow the process.

The traditional view is that strategy is concerned with making predictions based on analysis. Predictions, and the analysis which forms them, lead to security. The bottom-line is not expansion, future growth or increased profitability – it is survival. The assumption is that growth and increased profits will naturally follow. If, by using strategy, we can increase our chances of predicting successful methods, then our successful methods will lead us to survival and perhaps even improvement. So, strategy is to do with getting it right or, as the more competitive would say, winning. Of course it is possible to win battles and lose wars and so strategy has also grown up in the context of linking together a series of actions with some longer-term goals or aims.

This was all very well in the 1960s and for much of the 1970s. Predictions and strategies were formed with confidence and optimism (though they were not necessarily implemented with such sureness). Security could be found. The business environment appeared to be reassuringly stable. Objectives could be set and strategies developed to meet them in the knowledge that the overriding objective would not change. This approach became known as Management By Objectives.

Management By Objectives (MBO) was about identifying a target and developing strategies to achieve it. Under MBO, strategy formulation is a conscious, rational process. The process is backed with hard data and analysis so that a single, right answer can be identified and a clear plan articulated. In practice, MBO demanded too much data. It became overly complex and also relied too heavily on the past to predict the future. The entire system was ineffective at handling, encouraging or adapting to change. MBO simplified management to a question of reaching A from B using as direct a route as possible. Under MBO, the ends justified the means. The managerial equivalent of highways were developed in order to reach objectives quickly with the minimum hindrance from outside forces.

'The confusion of means and ends characterizes our age,' Henry Mintzberg observes and, today, the highways are liable to be gridlocked. When the highways are blocked managers are left to negotiate minor country roads to reach their objectives. And then comes the final confusion: the destination is likely to have changed during the journey. Equally, while MBO sought to narrow objectives and ignore all other forces, success (the objective) is now less easy to identify. Today's measurements of success can include everything from environmental performance to meeting equal opportunities targets. Success has expanded beyond the bottom line.

> Planning by its very nature defines and preserves categories. Creativity, by its very nature, creates categories or rearranges established ones. This is why strategic planning can neither provide creativity, nor deal with it when it emerges by other means.
>
> **Henry Mintzberg**

Another fatal flaw in the conventional view of strategy is that it tended to separate the skills required to develop strategy in the first place (analytical) from those needed to achieve its objectives in reality (practical). The divide between analysis and practice is patently artificial. Strategy does not stop and start, it is a continuous process of redefinition and implementation.

When the future could be expected to follow neat linear patterns, strategy had a clear place in the order of things. Now, the neatness is being upset, new perspectives are necessary. Even attitudes to time are being questioned. Western admiration of the Chinese economic renaissance makes Eastern notions of time intriguing – the East tends to use a cyclical conception of time which is not driven by achievement or by short-term objectives. Instead, it is deterministic and fatalistic.

If time can be questioned – or, at least, our perception of time – nothing is sacred and, corporations must constantly wrestle with fundamental issues. While accepting that every company needs a strategy – either explicit or implicit – it is increasingly recognized that expressing a need for strategy does not help to determine what strategy actually is or entails.

Resources

Alessandro Di Fiore's articles are at ecsi-consulting.com

On war #18

Karl von Clausewitz (1780–1831) was a Prussian general and military strategist. Von Clausewitz fought in the Napoleonic wars and in the Rhine campaigns (1793–94). Then, working on behalf of Russia from 1812 until 1814, von Clausewitz helped negotiate the convention of Tauroggen (1812). This laid the ground for an alliance of Prussia, Russia, and Great Britain in opposition to Napoleon. In his later career, von Clausewitz rejoined the Prussian army, fought at the Battle of Waterloo, and became director of the Prussian war college in 1818. His book, *On War*, was unfinished and published posthumously.

Von Clausewitz was firmly of the mind that comparisons between the military and commercial worlds were both valid and useful.

'Rather than comparing it [war] to art we could more accurately compare it to commerce, which is also a conflict of interests and activities; and it is still closer to politics, which in turn may be considered as a kind of commerce on a larger scale,' he writes in *On War*. As one would expect of a military theorist, von Clausewitz possesses a strong strain of pragmatism.

'To be practical, any plan must take account of the enemy's power to frustrate it; the best chance of overcoming such obstruction is to have a plan that can be easily varied to fit the circumstances met; to keep such adaptability, while still keeping the initiative, the best way is to operate along a line which offers alternative objectives,' he advises.

Mere theory will get you nowhere. (In this, and other areas, von Clausewitz was heavily influenced by the wily, power politics so potently mapped out by Machiavelli.) 'Knowing is different from doing and therefore theory must never be used as norms for a standard, but merely as aids to judgement,' von Clausewitz writes. Pragmatism is combined with a desire to achieve results through minimal effort – 'A prince or general can best demonstrate his genius by managing a campaign exactly to suit his objectives and his resources, doing neither too much nor too little.'

Most famously, von Clausewitz observes that war 'is merely the continuation of policy by other means'. Instead of being catastrophic, he views war as a normal and acceptable part of politics. Little wonder, perhaps, that Mao and Lenin were fans of von Clausewitz's work.

Von Clausewitz differentiates between strategy – the overall plan – and mere tactics – planning of a discrete part of the overall plan (i.e. the battle). Above this, von Clausewitz placed what he labeled 'grand strategy', the overall political aims. Arguments over the difference between strategy and tactics have raged inconclusively ever since.

Von Clausewitz's view was that success came through concentrating on one battle at a time. This is the distant precursor of the managerial theory of Management By Objectives. 'By looking on each engagement as part of a series, at least insofar as events are predictable, the commander is always on the high road to his goal,' he writes.

> Strategy is the art of making use of time and space. I am less chary of the latter than the former; space we can recover, time never.
>
> **Napoleon Bonaparte, ambitious soldier**

More recently management thinkers have sought inspiration from leading military thinker Basil Liddell Hart (1895–1970) – in particular from his 1967 book, *Strategy*. And, today's management gurus – including Richard Pascale – have examined military approaches to such issues as leadership, training, motivation and strategy.

Indeed, von Clausewitz has undergone something of a renaissance. A 2001 book, *Clausewitz on Strategy: Inspiration and Insight from a Master Strategist*, gathered a selection of his bon mots. The selection was made by consultants from the Boston Consulting Group and an academic from the US's National War College.

While Clausewitz's insights are interesting – especially for nineteenth-century Prussian military enthusiasts – their usefulness is debatable. Traditional military role models look increasingly tired and out of kilter with business reality. Across the world there is a move away from military role models which essentially exercise control on not only team-members' behaviors but also on their thinking. For companies to survive in this increasingly competitive global world it is essential to have front-line people who can think for themselves and exercise a high degree of creativity. The traditional military model of command and control mitigates against this.

'Obviously there will be some aspects of military leadership that are applicable to the leadership of today – trust and precision for example,' says Fons Trompenaars, co-author of *21 Leaders for the 21st Century*. 'However, in the military I have seen a lot of extravagances go unpunished because of the simplicity of the goal or the enemy. In the modern business world things are more complex than having just one adversary.' It seems that even a well-thumbed copy of *On War* is unlikely to be of use if the entire world is out to compete with you.

Resources

Karl von Clausewitz, *On War* (trans. and ed. Michael Howard and Peter Paret), Princeton University Press, 1984.

Tiha von Ghyczy, Bolko von Oetinger and Christopher Bassford (eds) *Clausewitz on Strategy*, John Wiley, 2001

Change while you are ahead #19

Columbia Business School's Rita McGrath told us:

> Stability is risky. By the time you need change management it's almost too late. You want to be in continual motion. There are some things you want to keep stable as an organization. You want stability in values, you want stability in leadership, you want stability in your core reason for being. And I actually found firms that were capable of super success in this very dynamic environment combined stability with motion. So they had a lot of stability in things like values and talent and networks and developing people, and incredible dynamism in investments and locations, how they move people around. And so it's this combination of stability with dynamism that seems to be the trick.

Dynamic stability is an elusive state. When do you perform a strategic volte-face and head in a new direction? The reality is that most organizations don't act until it is too late. The time to question your strategy and change things is usually now.

After all, the only surefire rule is that competitive advantages change. Yesterday's competitive advantage is history. Intel's Andy Grove wrote a great book entitled *Only the Paranoid Survive* and former H-P chief Lew Platt suggested that H-P should stand for 'healthy paranoia' and explained why:

> General Motors, Sears, International Business Machines, were the greatest companies in their industries, the best of the best in the world. These companies did not make gigantic mistakes. They were not led by stupid, inept people. The only real mistake they made was to keep doing what it was that had made them successful for a little too long.

It doesn't have to be that way. Consider the clothing retailer Benetton. In 1992 it had a turnover in excess of £1 billion and appeared to have the world at its feet. Luciano Benetton disagreed and decided that the company needed to embrace the future before it was too late. The company changed the way it did business.

At the time, Benetton was (according to the company at least) the third best known brand in the world. But Luciano Benetton wanted to move the company forward. At the company's headquarters in Ponzano Veneto, a seventeenth-century villa just outside Castrette di Villorba, north of Venice, Benetton came up with a highly ambitious plan. In response to high labor costs, Benetton invested a massive £80 million in an advanced clothing factory. It installed state of the art systems – software told the machines what to make in response to information coming directly from the company's stores worldwide.

> Companies don't produce strategies, just plans.
>
> **Gary Hamel**

Its investment in technology made Benetton's Castrette industrial complex among the world's most advanced. The factory was soon producing almost 100 million garments every year and included an automatic distribution system handling over 30,000 packages every day. This process was managed by a mere 19 people – a traditional system required at least 400.

Benetton's support systems and studious awareness of how it was pushing and pulling its brand mean that, in Benetton's case, bigger did actually become better.

And the strategic lessons?

One, keep it simple. Benetton's trademark products – colorful clothing – are strikingly simple but instantly recognizable as the company's. It has extended its interests with caution. Its other brands now include Zerotondo, Sisley and 012. It moved into sportswear and sporting equipment through such brands as Prince, Nordica and Rollerblade.

Two, attract attention. The 'United Colors of Benetton' brand provides a large variety of easy options for advertising images. Eschewing them, Benetton has cornered the market in surprising, or offensive, advertising. One featured Luciano Benetton naked except for the line 'I want my clothes back'. Then there are the shocking images of people dying. Gratuitous? Perhaps, but it has largely succeeded in cementing Benetton's niche as a colorful outsider.

Photographer Oliviero Toscani has been responsible for some of the most striking images used by Benetton. 'Everything we do is about impulse, about guts,' says Toscani. 'That's what built Benetton; Luciano didn't test the market for a taste in colored sweaters.' The ads are an expression of the brand, of the company and of Luciano Benetton.

This is how the company explains the images it uses to sell more sweaters:

> Benetton's communication strategy was born of the company's wish to produce images of global concern for its global customers... Benetton believes that it is important for companies to take a stance in the real world instead of using their advertising budget to perpetuate the myth that they can make consumers happy through the mere purchase of their product.

True enough, but Benetton's 'stance' is often difficult to determine.

Change while you are ahead. Often stated; rarely achieved.

Emerging thinkers on strategy #20

Rita McGrath

Rita McGrath is a professor at Columbia Business School. She is regarded as one of the world's top experts on strategy and innovation with particular emphasis on developing sound strategy in uncertain and volatile environments.

She is the author and co-author (with Ian MacMillan) of a number of best-selling books. These include: *The Entrepreneurial Mindset* (Harvard Business School Press, 2000); *Market Busters* (Harvard Business School Press, 2005); and *Discovery Driven Growth* (Harvard Business School Press, 2008).

McGrath won the 2013 Thinkers50 Strategy Award; and her most recent book *The End of Competitive Advantage: How to Keep Your Strategy Moving as Fast as Your Business* (HBSP, 2013) was shortlisted for the Thinkers50 Best Book Award. In it, she convincingly sounds the death knell for sustainable competitive advantage, arguing that strategy and innovation are converging.

McGrath argues that it's time to go beyond the very concept of sustainable competitive advantage. Instead, organizations need to forge a new path to winning: capturing opportunities fast, exploiting them decisively, and moving on even before they are exhausted. She shows how to do this with a new set of practices based on the notion of transient competitive advantage.

Her ideas are widely used by leading organizations throughout the world, including many Fortune 500 companies. Her thinking is described as sometimes provocative, but unfailingly stimulating. She fosters a fresh approach to strategy among those with whom she works.

She has also been inducted into the Strategic Management Society 'Fellows' in recognition of her impact on the field.

Sangeet Paul Choudary

'A new business model that uses technology to connect people, organizations and resources in an interactive ecosystem in which amazing amounts of value can be created and exchanged.' That is the definition of a platform as outlined by Sangeet Paul Choudary. Think Uber, Airbnb, Alibaba and Facebook.

This brave new world of platform business models and multi-sided network effects is explained by Choudary in two books *Platform Revolution* (with Geoffrey Parker and Marshall Van Alstyne) and *Platform Scale*. His latest thinking is available via his Platform Thinking blog (www.platformed.info).

Choudary's speaking focuses on four topics: the platform revolution; the changing geometry of business; the interaction economy; and the race for attention.

Choudary is the Founder and CEO of Platform Thinking Labs. He is also the co-chair of the MIT Platform Strategy Summit at MIT Media Labs, Boston, an Entrepreneur-in-Residence at INSEAD Business School, a Global Fellow at the Center for Global Enterprise in New York, and an advisor at 500 Startups in Silicon Valley.

Alessandro Di Fiore

Alessandro Di Fiore is the Founder and CEO of ECSI, a management research and executive education center as well as a consulting firm. He focuses on generating new management thinking and advising clients on the application of leading edge management tools and techniques. He is a frequent Harvard Business Review blogger on innovation and strategy.

ECSI's motto is 'resist the usual,' and the company prides itself on its cutting-edge research. Di Fiore championed the concept of the fifteen-word strategy statement as a tool to help business leaders focus on and communicate their strategic intent. The tool was the subject of an HBR blog ('How to Execute a 15-Word Strategy Statement', 2014).

More recently he has looked at the need to market your innovation activities as well as actually innovating and has championed the insight-driven organization. Says Di Fiore:

> The reality is that innovation is a battle which has to be fought on two fronts. First, companies have to develop their innovation capabilities. The second front is the world of appearances. Compared to developing innovation capabilities, innovation marketing is neglected. But, our research suggests that it is vital. Investors need to be informed and convinced of a company's ability to continue to innovate far into the future. This means being able to build a thought leadership profile on innovation, be known and perceived as an innovative company at the leading edge in your industry.

It is not enough to be innovative, you have to be seen to be.

Before ECSI, Di Fiore worked for more than twenty years in management consulting, initially in large international groups before founding a European strategy boutique called Venture Consulting. He sold Venture Consulting to Tefen, an international management consulting company floated on the Tel Aviv stock exchange.

Di Fiore is chairman of *Harvard Business Review Italia*. He holds a Master of Science in Economics & Business from Federico II University in Italy and has earned the PPL (President Program in Leadership) at Harvard Business School. He was the European Educational Chair for YPO-WPO (www.ypo.org), the largest business leaders' association in the world.

Alex Osterwalder

Alex Osterwalder is a Swiss business theorist, author, consultant, and passionate entrepreneur, who co-founded Strategyzer, a software company specializing in tools and content for strategic management and innovation. He is famous for his work on business modeling and the development of the Business Model Canvas.

Osterwalder is the lead author of the international best-seller *Business Model Generation: A Handbook for Visionaries, Gamechangers and Challengers* (Wiley, 2010). The book, co-authored with Yves Pigneur, is based on a tool called the Business Model Canvas, and is now available in thirty languages. Aimed at start-ups and companies that want to redesign or re-evaluate their business model, the Business Model Canvas allows companies to design, test, build and manage business models. It is used by household-name companies including Coca Cola, General Electric, Procter & Gamble, Mastercard, Ericsson, Lego and 3M.

> Strategies are okayed in boardrooms that even a child would say are bound to fail. The problem is, there is never a child in the boardroom.
>
> **Victor Palmieri, turnaround expert**

The book features a highly visual, four-color design that explains a range of strategic ideas and tools, and the content was co-created with practitioners from 45 countries through 470 Business Model Canvases.

Osterwalder and Pigneur followed the success of Business Model Generation with a string of other books, including: *Value Proposition Design: How to Create Products and Services Customers Want*; and *Business Model You: A One-Page Model for Reinventing Your Career.*

Gary Pisano

Gary Pisano is a Harvard Business School professor, co-author of *Producing Prosperity* (HBR, 2012) and most recently author of the influential *Harvard Business Review* article 'You Need an Innovation Strategy'.

Pisano is the Harry E. Figgie Professor of Business Administration at Harvard Business School. Pisano's research, teaching and consulting focus on technology strategy, the management of innovation and intellectual property, competitive strategy, and manufacturing and outsourcing strategy. His work on these issues spans a range of science and technology-based industries including aerospace, biotechnology and pharmaceuticals, specialty chemicals, health care, nutrition, computers, software, telecommunications and semiconductors.

He is the author of six books including *The Development Factory*; *Operations, Strategy, and Technology*; *Science Business: The Promise, The Reality and The Future of Biotech*; and, most recently, *Producing Prosperity: Why America Needs a Manufacturing Renaissance*.

He is also the author of over 70 articles and case studies. His 'Restoring American Competitiveness' (co-authored with Willy Shih) won the McKinsey Award for best article published in *Harvard Business Review* in 2009. He is also co-author of the award-winning article, 'Dynamic Capabilities and Strategic Management' (*Strategic Management Journal*, 1997), one of the most widely cited publications in economics and business since 1995.

Pisano's article 'How to Capture Value from Innovation: Shaping Intellectual Property and Industry Architecture' (*California Management Review*) was a finalist for the 2008 Accenture Award.

He serves as an advisor to senior executives at leading companies throughout the world and is a co-founder, along with chemistry Nobel Laureate Richard Schrock and others, of XiMo AG, a developer of specialty catalysts for the pharmaceutical and fine chemicals industries (www.ximo-inc.com).

From Boston with a matrix #21

'It struck me that if you look at strategy as an intellectual construct, a framework, a set of ideas, it really didn't exist in a formal way much before the 1960s,' observes Walter Kiechel in *The Lords of Strategy: The Secret History of the New Corporate World*.

Until the 1960s, models were the impenetrable domain of economists. The man who can be largely credited with bringing business models into the mainstream was Bruce Henderson (1915–92). Henderson was an engineer who worked as a strategic planner for General Electric. He was also dismissive of economists – 'Darwin is probably a better guide to business competition than economists are,' said Henderson. From GE, he joined the management consultancy, Arthur D. Little. In 1963, Henderson announced that he was leaving to set up his own consultancy, the Boston Consulting Group (BCG).

At the time, management consulting was beginning to establish itself as a profession and BCG is regarded by some as the first pure strategy consultancy. While strategy drifts in and out of fashion, it is a cause which BCG still robustly champions. 'Strategy leads to the continuous creation of real value. Real value requires sustained competitive advantage. Leaping at opportunities without strategy consistently produces failure,' it says. BCG quickly became a great success. Within five years it was in the top group of consulting firms – where it has largely remained. It has been called 'the most idea driven major consultancy in the world'.

The first model discovered – or re-discovered in this case – by Henderson was something of an antique. In the 1920s, an obscure company called Curtiss Aircraft came up with the concept of the 'learning curve', which also became known as the 'experience curve'. This posited that unit costs declined as cumulative production increased because of the acquisition of experience. This had been applied solely to manufacturing. Henderson applied it to strategy rather than production and found that it still worked and provided a useful practical tool.

BCG went on to originate or develop concepts such as sustainable growth; time-based competition; Segment-of-One marketing; value-based strategy; total shareholder value; and, even, disease management. However, the model for which Henderson and BCG are best known is the Boston Matrix which measures market growth and relative market share for all the businesses in a particular firm. The hypothesis of the Boston Matrix is that companies with higher market share in faster growing industries are more profitable. The further to the left a business is on the Boston Matrix, the stronger a company should be.

> Strategic planning, at best, is about posing questions, more than attempting to answer them.
>
> **Richard Pascale, academic, consultant and author**

As with most such models, refinements have been added along the way. On its original matrix, BCG superimposed a theory of cash management which included a hierarchy of uses of cash, numbered from one to four in their order of priority. This identified the top priority as cash cows, characterized by high market share and low growth. Investment in cash cows is easily justified as they are dull, safe and highly profitable. Next in line are the stars (high growth; high market share) though their investment requirements are likely to be significant. More problematic is the third category, question marks (or wildcats in some versions) where there is high growth and low share. Any investment in them is risky. The final category is the aptly titled, dogs, where low market share is allied to low growth. Dogs should not be approached.

Bruce Henderson was something of a legend as an employer. One of his recruits was Peter Lampl, now Sir Peter, founder of the Sutton Trust. 'When I joined BCG, it was the best management consulting firm in the world. I was the first person to join BCG in Boston directly from a European business school. And I was treated like dirt! It had a total free market system. So, I arrived at BCG in 1973. I didn't know anyone. They said, there's your desk. And I said, well, what do I do? I was told that I had to find work, I had to talk to managers and vice-presidents and get them to employ me. I had a pretty tough start,' Lampl told us.

> The whole measure of performance at BCG was billability – how many hours you bill clients each week. That's all that mattered. Bruce Henderson had a chart up in the office where everyone's monthly billability was listed, as well as their moving annual billability, so you could see every month how everybody was doing. If people were declining in billability, they would disappear. All of a sudden, they wouldn't show up. There was a huge churn rate, a half-life of about two and a half years. Bruce believed in survival of the fittest. It was crazy, but unbelievably exciting. At that time BCG was leading the pack. We were developing portfolio strategy, the experience curve and so on. We had some wonderful assignments.

Celebrated in the 1960s, the Boston Matrix proved a highly popular innovation. From a business point of view, the Matrix had the characteristics of any great model: it was accessible, simple and useful. However, it was also limiting. Measuring corporate performance against two parameters is straightforward, but potentially dangerous if these are the only two parameters against which performance is measured. A creature of its times, the Matrix offered a blinkered view of a world where growth and profitability were all.

The Boston Matrix encouraged a preoccupation with market share. This was not to the liking of all executives. In a 1974 speech, David Packard warned Hewlett-Packard staff: 'If I hear anybody talking about how big their share of the market is or what they're trying to do to increase their share of the market, I'm going to personally see that a black mark gets put in their personnel folder.'

Not surprisingly, other consulting firms were quick to respond with their own variations on the Boston Matrix. The most credible response came in the form of the General Electric and McKinsey matrix. This measured performance against two variables – industry attractiveness and business strength – and was effectively a dandified version of the original.

As a business tool, the Boston Matrix had a significant and long-term impact. It provides a useful way of looking at the world. Of equal significance was its influence on the management consulting business. It spawned a host of imitators. Now, no consultant's report is complete without a matrix of some sort. More importantly, BCG effectively introduced off-the-shelf consulting (though it wouldn't see it that way). Companies required the company's big idea. They wanted to see how they fared on the Matrix and how it could shape their strategies. The consulting firm product was born.

Previously consultants had gone in to client companies to solve specific business problems. The success of the Boston Matrix marked a change in tack. As well as problem solving, consultancy became concerned with passing on the latest ideas, the frameworks, models and matrices which were the height of fashion. Problem solvers became peddlers of big ideas. This opened up huge new vistas for the management consultancy profession which it has been assiduously – and profitably – chasing ever since.

Resources

Walter Kiechel, *The Lords of Strategy*, Harvard Business Press, 2010.

Strategic nations #22

Eventually, strategists feel cramped by coming up with neat strategies for corporations – however multinational they might be. They crave a bigger stage. Michael Porter has tackled strategy in the health-care industry – notably in a series of articles co-authored with Harvard colleague Mark Kramer. Porter has also squared the capitalist circle by showing how companies can combine their competitive instincts with social responsibility and other activities that while socially beneficial do not appear to contribute to shareholder value.

Perhaps Porter's most successful foray into other corners of the strategy world was his work on competition and countries. His 1990 book, *The Competitive Advantage of Nations*, must be ranked as one of the most ambitious books of our times. At its heart was a radical new perspective on the role and *raison d'être* of nations. Porter charted their transformation from being military powerhouses to economic units whose competitiveness is the key to power and influence.

Richard D'Aveni is another strategy thinker who has continued to find new facets of strategy to explore. Most recently, in his 2012 book *Strategic Capitalism*, he scaled up the target of his strategic analysis. Like Porter and number of other strategists before him, D'Aveni has shifted his unit of analysis from business or firm, to government and nation, and ultimately to entire economic systems. Thus, in the book he is concerned with hypercompetition between various forms of capitalism, and the economic power struggle between nations and economic power blocs. In particular, D'Aveni is interested in the different models of capitalism being pursued by the US and China.

The word iconoclast is overused, but not in the case of Richard D'Aveni. D'Aveni is a contrarian. One of the reasons we like his work is that he looks at the world differently and dares to challenge the orthodoxy. His analysis is controversial. It is as provocative as it is refreshingly unflinching.

D'Aveni notes that a constant stream of headlines from China indicate that corporate America is under attack. When we talked to him he pointed to two examples: the Bo Xilai scandal – a story that illustrated how business interests in China are tied up with affairs of the state. The second was that the Fed had just approved three state-owned Chinese banks to move into US markets. D'Aveni told us with characteristic gusto:

> A strategy is no good if people don't fundamentally believe in it.
>
> **Robert Haas, businessman**

> What we are witnessing, in my view, is an escalation from competition between corporations to competition between nations. The struggle between China and the US amounts to the opening moves of a Capitalist Cold War. With the rise of the new economic powerhouses, especially China, we are seeing a new form of capitalism where states compete against other states – or more accurately their forms of capitalism compete with each other for economic success.

D'Aveni describes the new reality as hypercompetition between nations. This new reality is characterized by 'a series of actions by rival nations seeking to tilt the playing field to their advantage – in effect to set the rules of competition. It also comprises moves and countermoves to disrupt or undermine the form of capitalism used by rivals. We have seen it before.'

D'Aveni points to corporate Japan's development in the 1970s and 1980s of a form of managed capitalism that featured domestic industry groups called keiretsu and informal zaibatsu (outlawed after World War Two). They sought not to maximize corporate profits in the short run;

they sought to maximize employment in Japan and reinvestment in the long-term growth of the groups. This brand of capitalism was not capitalism as practiced and understood in the West.

So, what can American and other Western companies do to raise their game, to understand the new strategic stakes? D'Aveni warns:

> Now is not the time to rely on ideological or theory-based ideas that encapsulate what used to work. Most ideologies and theories are not appropriate anymore. They freeze our thinking, paralyze our ability to adjust, and doom American companies to continued deadlock and decline. Only a fool continues doing the same thing and expects different results. In *Strategic Capitalism*, I urge America's business leaders to look at the future strategically, and to craft a strategy for winning over the long term. It does not promote ideology, whether from the left, right, or center. It promotes pragmatic thinking that comes from anyone with good ideas.

Resources

Richard D'Aveni, *Strategic Capitalism*, McGraw Hill, 2012.

Mintzberg on strategy #23

The work of Canadian Henry Mintzberg counters much of the detailed rationalism of other major thinkers of recent decades. From his first publication, *The Nature of Managerial Work*, Mintzberg has challenged orthodoxy, arguing the case for a more intuitive and humane approach to strategy formulation and practice, as well as the structure of organizations. *The Nature of Managerial Work* exposed many of the myths surrounding senior managers, revealing them to be creatures of the moment rather than far-sighted strategists carefully planning their next move.

Mintzberg has generated a unique reputation, as someone apart from the mainstream able to analyze basic assumptions about managerial behavior. His most recent work tackles head-on the role and process of strategic planning. Mintzberg argues that intuition is 'the soft underbelly of management' and that strategy has set out to provide uniformity and formality where none can be created.

Mintzberg emphasizes the creative and spontaneous, the right-side of the brain rather than the left-side with its predilection for analysis and rationality. He is a wry humanist who carries out his work with academic rigor. 'A well published waif' is how he jokingly describes himself; 'perhaps the world's premier management thinker,' says Tom Peters.

There is a sizeable dose of cynicism in Mintzberg's worldview. Though, when asked, he is quick to add the explanatory coda: 'I am skeptical about everything except reality.' To keep hold of reality, he eschews the management guru merry-go-round. He says:

> There is a lot of obnoxious hype about being a 'guru' to the extent that the medium can destroy the message. I'm in one of the most competitive fields around, but I've never felt competition for a moment. You can compete by competing head on or by not competing at all. I care about doing things well, not doing them better – that is a low standard.

Mintzberg's name was initially brought to a wider audience with his first book, *The Nature of Managerial Work* (1973). An article in the *Harvard Business Review* ('The Manager's Job: Folklore and Fact') brought Mintzberg's research further into the public eye. Its origins (and those of subsequent books) lie in Mintzberg's grand plan. 'In 1968, I set out to write a text called The Theory of Management Policy, to draw together the research-based literature that helps to describe the processes of general management.' Mintzberg's plan has expanded – each of the three central chapters became books and an early section of the fourth chapter also developed into a book.

At the time of its publication, *The Nature of Managerial Work* was radically alternative and rapidly dispensed with much conventional wisdom. 'I had a lot of difficulty getting my first book published,' Mintzberg recalls. 'One publisher said they were publishing a book just like it – twenty years later, I have yet to see the book.' In his research, Mintzberg got close to managers actually managing rather than pontificating from afar. His research involved spending time with five organizations and analyzing how their chief executives spent their time. While this tracking approach is now commonplace, in the early 1970s it was ambitious – previous research had concentrated on the people managed by managers and the structure of organizations rather than the day-to-day reality of managerial behavior and performance.

Mintzberg's style and approach has remained determinedly iconoclastic. 'My books succeeded because they were different,' he says. 'If you think differently and execute it poorly you are dead.'

His background in mechanical engineering might explain the root of Mintzberg's techniques and thinking. 'Mechanical engineering is not concerned with image or status. It is about reality and requires a certain kind of thinking,' he says, recalling a college assignment to design a pump. While all the other students went away and looked at the latest catalogs to copy a design, Mintzberg didn't look at anything and came up with a pump virtually identical to those pumps when they were first invented. In his later research, Mintzberg also seeks to reinvent or establish first principles for himself. He says:

> I am not an intellectual. I am a writer and researcher. I write primarily for myself, to find things out. I never write anything to boost my reputation or image – sometimes it is appropriate to publish something in the *Harvard Business Review*. When I am writing the painful stage is getting an outline and then there is joy when things click and integrate.

At the core of Mintzberg's work is a belief in the excitement and spontaneity of management and faith in people rather than organizations – 'I don't like to be organized – I am a voyeur'. He has little time for the formal dictates of the organization. 'We have become prisoners of cerebral management. I'm sympathetic to the management process which is intuitive, based on immediate responses,' he says. Instead of seeing strategy as the apotheosis of rationalism Mintzberg has famously coined the term 'crafting strategy', whereby strategy is created as deliberately, delicately and dangerously as a potter making a pot. To Mintzberg strategy is more likely to 'emerge', through a kind of organizational osmosis, than be produced by a group of strategists sitting round a table believing they can predict the future.

Mintzberg's later work is probably his most controversial. 'Strategy is not the consequence of planning but the opposite: its starting point,' he says, countering the carefully wrought arguments of strategists, from Igor Ansoff in the 1960s to the Boston Consulting Group in the 1970s and Michael Porter in the 1980s. *The Rise and Fall of Strategic Planning* is a masterly and painstaking deconstruction of the central pillars of management theory. Mintzberg exposes the fallacies and failings at the root of planning. These include:

- Processes – a fascination with elaborate processes creates bureaucracy and strangles innovation.

- Data – Mintzberg argues that 'hard' data, the lifeblood of the traditional strategist, is a source of information; 'soft' data, however, provides the wisdom. 'Hard information can be no better and is often at times far worse than soft information,' he writes. In *The Nature of Managerial Work*, Mintzberg similarly observed that managers relied on 'soft information' rather than exhaustive written reports.
- Detachment – Mintzberg refutes the notion of managers creating strategic plans from ivory towers. 'Effective strategists are not people who abstract themselves from the daily detail but quite the opposite: they are the ones who immerse themselves in it, while being able to abstract the strategic messages from it.'

Looking at the development of his work, Mintzberg observes: 'My perception of what constitutes effective management is not so different as it was. But now there is a lot more ineffective management.' In *The Rise and Fall of Strategic Planning*, he produces a typical paragraph (on the role of the effective strategist) which has the air of someone thinking aloud, but perhaps sums up Mintzberg's own approach:

> Perceiving the forest from the trees is not the right metaphor at all … because opportunities tend to be hidden under the leaves. A better one may be to detect a diamond in the rough in a seam of ore. Or to mix the metaphors, no one ever found a diamond by flying over a forest. From the air, a forest looks like a simple carpet of green, not the complex living system it really is.

Resources

Henry Mintzberg's books include *The Nature of Managerial Work*, Harper & Row, 1973; *The Structuring of Organizations*, Prentice-Hall, 1979; *Mintzberg on Management*, Free Press, 1989); and *The Rise and Fall of Strategic Planning*, Prentice Hall International, 1994.

Innovating strategy #24

IBM made $6 billion in 1990 and lost $5 billion two years later. The company, one of the twentieth-century's corporate greats, failed to change with the market and only moved when value had well and truly migrated.

Over any period the needs and expectations of customers change. If a company fails to keep pace, it will find itself left behind. This is the essence of the idea of value migration, defined by Adrian Slywotzky, Richard Tedlow and Benson Shapiro as 'the flow of economic and shareholder value away from obsolete business models to new, more effective designs'.

To gain an insight into value migration, Shapiro, Tedlow and Slywotzky suggest that companies ask themselves a number of questions. These begin with 'List your most important product and customer service attributes for five years in the future, for today and for five years ago', and also cover market share, percentage of new product failures and ratio of profit from new products. Honest answers to the questions provide a sense of how your company is positioned in terms of value migration. Warning lights flash, for example, if your customers' business is shrinking, if the quality of your market share is declining or if your profits from new products are low.

In response to the flashing lights, a company can do a variety of things. It may examine the value migration process within its industry; look more intensely at trends in customer needs; or make comparisons with the structure of competitors. Moving early is essential. Instead of being reduced to a panic-stricken burst of downsizing, Shapiro, Tedlow and Slywotzky suggest that companies should gradually shift investment away from the old design; invest in new capabilities; and protect the new businesses.

The trouble is that changing or evolving strategy is a difficult task, especially if a strategy appears to be working.

Costas Markides defines strategic innovation as 'a fundamental reconceptualization of what the business is all about which in turn leads to a dramatically different way of playing the game in our existing business'.

Markides argues that such innovation is achieved by a small number of organizations. The number of innovators is so small due to a combination of structural and cultural inertia. Companies generally have little appetite for true innovation, strategic or otherwise.

Strategic innovation occurs when a company identifies a gap in the way it is positioned in a market, moves to fill the gap and uncovers a new mass market. Markides describes 'gaps' in three ways – as 'new customer segments emerging; or existing customer segments which are, however, neglected by existing competitors'; 'new customer needs emerging; or existing customer needs which are, however, not served well by existing competitors'; and 'new ways of producing, delivering or distributing existing (or new) products/services to existing (or new) customer segments'.

> Strategy is not the consequence of planning but the opposite: its starting point.
>
> **Henry Mintzberg**

To move to strategic innovation, Markides suggests a number of techniques. First, companies have to be prepared to ask basic questions of the way they currently do business. Successful companies find this almost impossible – profits tend to blunt their willingness to confront potential future difficulties. Strategic innovators, however, are able to ask questions. This Markides attributes to two reasons. First, they 'monitored not only their financial health but also their strategic health'. Suggestions that their strategies were coming adrift were speedily picked up on. Second, 'they artificially created a positive crisis to galvanize the organization into active thinking'.

Strategic innovators were also more adept at challenging existing strategic planning processes. 'Established companies are constantly preoccupied with how they need to compete in their business without ever questioning the who and the what of their business,' Markides laments. Questions lead to tomorrow's strategic answers.

Resources

Benson Shapiro, Adrian J. Slywotzky and Richard S. Tedlow, 'How to stop bad things happening to good companies', *Strategy & Business*, Issue 6 Spring 1997.

Gary Hamel, 'Strategy innovation and the quest for value', *Sloan Management Review*, Winter 1998.

Constantinos Markides, 'Strategic innovation: the leader's dilemma', *Sloan Management Review* Spring 1998.

New realities of strategy #25

On his journey around the wilds of strategic management in *Strategy Safari* (co-authored with Joseph Lampel), Henry Mintzberg identifies ten different schools of strategy formation.

The first five are: design – fitting internal situation of the organization with the external environment; planning – formal planning from analysis of situation to strategy execution; positioning – influenced by the ideas of Michael Porter – strategy depends on the positioning of the firm in the market and within its industry; entrepreneurial – strategy driven by the leader; and cognitive – delving inwards into the minds of strategists.

The second five are: learning – strategy as an emergent process – as people come to understand a situation and the organization's ability to deal with it strategy emerges; power – strategy from power games inside and outside the organization; cultural – the formation of strategy is tied to the social force of culture; environmental – strategy dependent on events in the environment and the company's reaction; and configuration – part of a transformational process.

The trouble is that, in practice, modern thinking about strategy does not fit neatly into one or another of the ten schools. More commonly, recent approaches to strategy formation cut across a number of the schools – whether it is resource-based thinking, chaos and evolutionary theory, revolutionary strategy, or strategic maneuvering. Neatness RIP.

Functional divides RIP

These are troubled times for the study and practice of strategy. Old truths are being relentlessly questioned. Neat divides are coming tumbling down.

As Columbia Business School's Rita McGrath told us:

> Strategy is really struggling both in the field and in the real world. You are seeing a bit of a gap. Porter's Five Forces, the BCG Matrix, SWOT analysis, a lot of those tools came from an era when competition was much less vigorous. They are great tools in the context in which they were developed. If you've got a stable industry structure and you've got things that you can actually measure they still work. But, today we're seeing industries competing with industries, different arenas where competition manifests itself. Strategy, entrepreneurship and innovation are all bleeding into each other.

There is functional blood on the ground.

Strategy embraces different points of view

Costas Markides of London Business School asks:

> What issues should senior executives consider in thinking about a new strategy and how should they think about them? Despite the apparent simplicity of this question, it is one of the most controversial in the field of management. As with most academic debates, when one probes below the surface, the apparently divergent points of view are in fact amazingly similar. Rather than depend on one perspective at the expense of all others, good strategies encompass elements from all the different perspectives and points of view.

The trouble is that in many corporations different points of view are notable by their absence. This is something Gary Hamel and C.K. Prahalad lamented in their work in the 1990s, arguing that strategy has tied itself into a straitjacket of narrow, and narrowing, perspectives: 'Among the people who work on strategy in organizations and the theorists, a huge proportion, perhaps 95 percent, are economists and engineers who share a mechanistic view of strategy. Where are the theologists, the anthropologists to give broader and fresher insights?' they asked. Where, indeed.

Hamel argues that it is only if we give greater consideration to the emergence of strategy that we will be able to create strategies which succeed.

Hamel maps out five preconditions for the emergence of strategy. First, the entire organization needs to have a voice in creating strategy. It is not the sole preserve of management but 'pluralistic and participative'. Second, discussion concerning strategy must cut across industries and organizations so that knowledge can be combined in new ways. Third, Hamel believes that people will embrace change when they identify opportunities for rewards and growth. (This also explains the redundancy of downsizing as a policy.) Finally, companies must carry out some market experimentation to determine which new strategies work.

> Unhappy the general who comes on the field of battle with a system.
>
> **Napoleon Bonaparte**

Strategy demands communication

Says Chris Zook of Bain & Co:

> It's interesting, I looked at a database recently of 300,000 employee surveys that were done with companies headquartered in Europe and one question that was asked was, do you have any idea what the company strategy is, what its priorities are and what makes it special? And only two out of five employees in the average business say they have any idea what that is. And if you imagine if you had a marching band or a football team where only two out of five knew the formation, that would be a problem; yet in the very best businesses, 85 percent of people say they really have an idea of what the business stands for. Whether it's a company like Nike that just jumps out at you as being about performance or Tetra Pak where it jumps

out at you being it's about the packaging, so often having a really simple and clear and powerful differentiation is the essence of it.

And very often, in the crush of daily pressure and life, executives and management teams find their time frittered away and spent by everything that comes up, every daily crisis, and this is even more true today, with the speed at which the world is changing. And so I think that the essence is that it's very hard to be really self-aware of what are the very few things that you are excellent at.

Strategy is improv

Stanford's Kathleen Eisenhardt has looked at the significance of improvisation in the strategic decision-making process. Eisenhardt argues that researchers into strategic decisions have tended to follow three basic approaches. First is what she labels, 'bounded rationality'. This approach ignores the influence of elements such as intuition, preferring a narrow, logic-based perspective. The second approach is termed 'power and politics'. This regards strategy as emerging from conflict and machinations among senior managers. Once again the emotional element is played down. The final approach is the 'garbage can'. This suggests that 'decision making occurs through the random meeting of choices looking for problems, decision makers looking for something to decide, problems looking for solutions, and so forth'. Once again this is only partly the case and certainly practically unhelpful.

Strategic decisions, Eisenhardt suggests, need a new and more dynamic model: improvisation. By improvisation she does not mean a spur of the moment free-for-all, but something altogether more structured. She says that true improvisation has two characteristics. The first is that it requires that people communicate intensely with each other. And such communication belongs to the moment. The second key characteristic is that 'improvisation involves performers relying on a few, very specific rules. There are not many rules, but those that do exist are religiously followed.'

Backed by research, improvisation is a convincing metaphor. The question must be, how helpful the metaphor can be in practice.

Strategy is messy

Henry Mintzberg is among those who have most loudly questioned the assumption that strategy making can be formalized. The left-side of the brain has dominated strategy formulation with its emphasis on logic and analysis. Overly structured, this creates a narrow range of options. Alternatives which do not fit into the predetermined structure are ignored. The right side of the brain needs to become part of the process with its emphasis on intuition and creativity. 'Planning by its very nature,' concludes Mintzberg, 'defines and preserves categories. Creativity, by its very nature, creates categories or rearranges established ones. This is why strategic planning can neither provide creativity, nor deal with it when it emerges by other means.'

World-changing strategies grow as freely as weeds in carefully tended gardens. Don't root them out but let them flourish.

Resources

Kathleen Eisenhardt, 'Strategic decisions and all that jazz', *Business Strategy Review*, Autumn 1997.

Keeping your balance #26

Over the last century measurement has lain at the heart of management. Indeed, measurement has often appeared to be the central function of management. Scientific Management, for example, involved measuring the performance of workers against predetermined optimum times. Managers have found different things to measure and more sophisticated means of measurement. And, as every manager knows, what gets measured gets done. The perennial problem for strategy has been that there is no obvious or meaningful means of measuring something so multifaceted and complex.

The most fruitful area for this mania for quantification has been finance. Managers once simply talked of sales and profits. But, over the years a complex array of ratios, measures, analytical tools and software packages have evolved. Every penny a company spends or produces can be analyzed in an infinite number of ways. Such are their powers of persuasion, that entire companies can be driven by such financial measures. The most famous instance of this was ITT in the 1960s under the control of Harold Geneen. Geneen took management by financial measurement to its limits, creating an elaborate system of financial reporting. When he left the company, the deck of cards collapsed.

The obvious conclusion to be drawn from Geneen's approach was that if you concentrated solely on financial measures, you could achieve short-term, even medium-term success, but such narrow constraining measures were unlikely to yield long-term prosperity. The trouble was that financial ratios and performance were the easiest things to measure.

Other elements of corporate performance – such as customer loyalty or employee satisfaction – were more abstract and measurement appeared to pose more questions than answers.

At the same time as companies were considering how to measure 'softer' elements of their performance, they became increasingly addicted to managerial fads and fashions.

So, organizations were faced with the dilemmas of unwieldy financial measurement systems; few reliable means of measuring other elements of their performance; and a predilection for short-lived fads whose impact is rarely measured in any way whatsoever.

The answer to these imbalances, proposed by David Norton and Robert Kaplan, was the Balanced Scorecard ('a strategic management and measurement system that links strategic objectives to comprehensive indicators'). Norton is co-founder of the consulting company, Renaissance Solutions, and Kaplan is Marvin Bower Professor of Leadership Development at Harvard Business School. The duo developed the Balanced Scorecard concept at the beginning of the 1990s in research sponsored by KPMG.

The result was an article in the *Harvard Business Review* ('The Balanced Scorecard', January/February 1993). This had a simple message for managers and one which probably sounded reassuringly familiar: what you measure is what you get. Kaplan and Norton compared running a company to flying a plane. The pilot who relies on a single dial is unlikely to be safe. Pilots must utilize all the information contained in their cockpit:

> The complexity of managing an organization today requires that managers be able to view performance in several areas simultaneously. Moreover, by forcing senior managers to consider all the important operational measures together, the balanced scorecard can let them see whether improvement in one area may be achieved at the expense of another.

Kaplan and Norton suggested that four elements need to be balanced. First is the customer perspective. Companies must ask how they are perceived by customers. The second element is 'internal perspective'. Companies must ask what it is that they must excel at. Third is the 'innovation and learning perspective'. Companies must ask whether they can continue to improve and create value. Finally is the financial perspective. How does the company look to shareholders?

According to Kaplan and Norton, by focusing energies, attention and measures on all four of these dimensions, companies become driven by their mission rather than by short-term financial performance. Crucial to achieving this is applying measures to company strategy. Instead of being beyond measurement, the Balanced Scorecard argues that strategy must be central to any process of measurement – 'A good Balanced Scorecard should tell the story of your strategy'.

Identifying the essential measures for an organization is not straightforward. One company produced 500 measures on its first examination. This was distilled down to seven measures – twenty is par for the course. According to Kaplan and Norton, a 'good' Balanced Scorecard contains three elements. First, it establishes 'cause and effect relationships'. Rather than being isolated figures, measures are related to each other and the network of relationships makes up the strategy. Second, a Balanced Scorecard should have a combination of lead and lag indicators. Lag indicators are measures, such as market share, which are common across an industry and, though important, offer no distinctive advantage. Lead indicators are measures which are company (and strategy) specific. Finally, an effective Balanced Scorecard is linked to financial measures. By this, Kaplan and Norton mean that initiatives such as re-engineering or lean production need to be tied to financial measures rather than pursued indiscriminately.

> Strategies are intellectually simple; their execution is not.
>
> **Larry Bossidy, industrialist**

In many ways, the concept of the Balanced Scorecard is brazen commonsense. Balance is clearly preferable to imbalance. (The counter intuitive reality is that unbalanced companies, usually driven by a single dominant individual, have often proved short-term successes.) The

Balanced Scorecard is now widely championed by a variety of companies. Indeed, it has somewhat ironically become a management fad. Its argument that blind faith in a single measurement or a small range of measures is dangerous is a powerful one. However, effective measures of elements, such as management competencies or intellectual capital, remain elusive.

Resources

Robert S. Kaplan and Robin Cooper, *Cost and effect: Using integrated cost systems to drive profitability and performance*, Harvard Business School Press, 1998.

Robert S. Kaplan and David P. Norton, *The Balanced Scorecard: Translating strategy into action*, Harvard Business School Press, 1996.

Not doing #27

Sometimes doing nothing is the best strategy. Simply, not doing.

When he became CEO in 1993, former McKinsey consultant and turnaround master, Lou Gerstner, decided not to split IBM – even though this was something which previous CEO, John Akers had prepared for. All or nothing was Gerstner's refrain. Gerstner reflected that IBM had been through 'an economic shock the equivalent of an earthquake'; another earthquake was the last thing it needed. Indeed, a vision was the last thing it needed. Nothing high falutin; just get on and manage was Gerstner's message.

And, under Gerstner, IBM made a surprisingly strong recovery. It got back in touch with reality and with its existing and potential customers. Take its role in Internet development. In 1993, long-serving IBM-er, John Patrick was arguing that everyone at the company should have their own email address and that the company needed a website. 'Connect with other people. If you become externally focused, you can change the whole company,' said Patrick. What is interesting is that Patrick's call to arms was basically a return to the company's first principles – get in touch with customers and communicate internally. The only difference was that Patrick was championing the latest technology to do so.

As proof that IBM's culture had changed, forces were mobilized in a way the slow moving monolith of the past never even contemplated. In 1995 only two of the company's 220,000 employees were working on Java. By 1997, 2,400 scientists and engineers throughout the world were doing so. Indeed, such is the cultural change that there was talk of breaking rules, using small eccentric groups to tackle problems from different angles, to bring fresh thinking, rather than the overconfidence of the past.

Lou Gerstner stalked in the background, pulling the strings, exerting pressure when needed. In fact, his behavior appeared to be a textbook example of modern leadership – empowering and coaching rather than controlling. At the same time, his feet appeared firmly planted in commercial reality. Said Gerstner: 'My view is you perpetuate success by continuing to run scared, not by looking back at what made you great, but looking forward at what is going to make you ungreat, so that you are constantly focusing on the challenges that keep you humble, hungry and nimble.'

> Unless structure follows strategy, inefficiency results.
>
> **Alfred Chandler, historian**

Typically, when Gerstner was shown the Internet for the first time his reaction was, 'This is great, this is a new channel for business. How do we make it real for customers? How do we make money on it?' The order of these priorities – customers and then profit – is perhaps the vital lesson from IBM's renaissance and the rise, fall and rise of the IBM brand.

And the strategic wisdom from the IBM story?

First, get in touch with customers and with reality. IBM had grown distant from the marketplace. Gerstner threw it back into the lion's den.

Second, togetherness may be strength. IBM could have been broken down into 100 significant organizations with 100 bright, new names. Gerstner's realization was that though this would have had some advantages, the continuing strength and resonance of the IBM brand name offset them.

Core thoughts #28

Gary Hamel recalls:

> By the 1990s strategy had become discredited. All too often 'vision' was ego masquerading as foresight; planning was formulaic, incrementalist and largely a waste of time in a world of discontinuous change; 'strategic' investments were those that lost millions, if not billions of dollars. As strategy professors, C.K. Prahalad and I had a simple choice: change jobs or try to reinvent strategy for a new age. We chose the latter course.

In their groundbreaking 1994 book, *Competing for the Future*, Hamel and Prahalad argue that strategy is multifaceted, emotional as well as analytical, concerned with meaning, purpose and passion. While strategy is a process of learning and discovery, it is not looked on as a learning process and this represents a huge blind spot.

Broader perspectives are necessitated by the 'emerging competitive reality' in which the onus is on transforming not just individual organizations but entire industries. The boldness of such objectives is put in perspective when Hamel and Prahalad observe that, for all the research and books on the subject, there remains no theory of strategy creation. Strategy emerges and the real problem, executives perceive, is not creating strategy but in implementing it. 'We have an enormous appetite for simplicity. We like to believe we can break strategy down to Five Forces or Seven Ss. But you can't. Strategy is extraordinarily emotional and demanding. It is not a ritual or a once-a-year exercise, though that is what it has become. We have set the bar too low,' say Hamel and Prahalad.

As a result, managers are bogged down in the nitty-gritty of the present – spending less than three percent of their time looking to the future.

Instead of talking about strategy or planning, they advocate that companies should talk of strategizing and ask 'What are the fundamental preconditions for developing complex, variegated, robust strategies?' Strategizing is part of the new managerial argot of 'strategic intent', 'strategic architecture', 'foresight' (rather than vision) and, crucially, the idea of 'core competencies'.

Hamel and Prahalad define core competencies as 'the collective learning in the organization, especially how to co-ordinate diverse production skills and integrate multiple streams of technologies' and call on organizations to see themselves as a portfolio of core competencies as opposed to business units. The former are geared to growing 'opportunity share' wherever that may be; the latter narrowly focused on market share and more of the same.

In some ways, Hamel and Prahalad's strategic prognosis falls between two extremes. At one extreme are the arch-rationalists, insisting on a constant stream of data to support any strategy; at the other are the 'thriving on chaos' school with their belief in freewheeling organizations where strategy is a moveable feast. There is a thin dividing line between order and chaos. They caution:

> Neither Stalinist bureaucracy nor Silicon Valley provide an optimal economic system. Silicon Valley is extraordinarily good at creating new ideas but in other ways is extraordinarily inefficient. There are 100 failures for every success and, in fact, you find that smaller companies usually succeed in partnership with large organizations.

They conclude that small entrepreneurial offshoots are not the route to organizational regeneration. They are too random, inefficient and prone to becoming becalmed by corporate indifference. This does not mean that interlopers can't change the shape of entire industries.

Hamel and Prahalad were also long-standing critics of the corporate obsession with downsizing, labeling it 'corporate anorexia'. The golden rules are summed up by Hamel and Prahalad: 'A company surrenders today's businesses when it gets smaller faster than it gets better. A company surrenders tomorrow's businesses when it gets better without getting different.' Downsizing is an easy option – 'There is nothing more short-term than a sixty year old CEO holding a fist full of share options.'

Growth (they prefer to talk of vitality) comes from difference; though they add the caveat that 'there are as many stupid ways to grow as there are to downsize. You might merge with another organization but two drunks don't make a sensible person.' The catch-22 for organizations is that vitality is usually ignited by a crisis – something borne out by the burgeoning literature on spectacular turnarounds.

> We all know a strategy when we see one.
>
> **Gary Hamel**

Perhaps reassuringly, Hamel and Prahalad believe vitality comes from within. If only executives would listen – 'Go to any company and ask when was the last time someone in their twenties spent time with the board teaching them something they didn't know. For many it is inconceivable, yet companies will pay millions of dollars for the opinions of McKinsey's bright 29-year old. What about their own 29-year olds?'

While such questions remain largely unanswered, Hamel and Prahalad are moving on to pose yet more: 'Something new needed to be said about the content of strategy. Now we need to rethink the process of strategy.'

Hamel's sequel *Leading the Revolution*, calls for companies to throw aside their single-strategy business plans and instead develop a deeply embedded capability for continual, radical innovation. Hamel now talks of 'creative strategizing'. By way of explanation he says:

> First, strategic planning is not strategy. Planning and strategic formulations are very different things. Strategy is discovering and inventing, which makes strategy subversive, and the strategist a rule-breaker, or revolutionary. Second, the real barrier to strategic planning is generally at the top, not in the middle nor at the bottom. The objective of the revolutionary is to free the process from

> the tyranny of the past. Its guardians are at the top. And, third, you cannot expect to see the end at the start. The strategic formulation is a discovery process and a moment of invention. It is not selling to those in the middle and at the bottom something already defined by those at the top or from outsiders (the external consultants).

For C.K. Prahalad the entire notion of core competencies was driven by his belief in the necessity of democratizing commerce. This is how he explained it to us:

> Think about core competencies as an idea. Core competence is not about top management; it's about ordinary workers, ordinary people, the ordinary technical community and the worker community working together to create intellectual capital. We are basically saying that intellectual capital is critical for companies to succeed, so don't underestimate the value added and the criticality of ordinary people. It's not all the top guys.

Resources

Gary Hamel and C.K. Prahalad, *Competing for the Future*, Harvard Business School Press, 1994.

Strategy breaks eggs #29

In 1952 Rupert Murdoch inherited the *Adelaide News and Sunday Mail* from his father. The *Adelaide News*, as left by Sir Keith Murdoch, was an uninspiringly small newspaper. The Murdoch inheritance was no empire. To it, Rupert brought youthful vigour and a willingness to embrace the mass market.

Murdoch took to business life easily. His life had been a preparation for it. From the very start, Murdoch began stretching his wings. As the ink dried and the presses whirled, deals were struck. In 1960, Murdoch bought the *Sydney Daily Mirror* and tested the water in the television market. Various deals came and went. Murdoch later explained the rationale behind his apparently indiscriminate purchasing: 'We tended to take the sick newspapers, the ones that weren't worth much, that people thought were about to fold up.' The purchases were backed by borrowing. Murdoch quickly learned that banks were only concerned about how reliably clients repaid their loans. Murdoch established a record of doing what he promised. Banks rolled over and offered more.

Perhaps the boldest sign of Murdoch's broadening ambitions was his founding of *The Australian*, the country's first national newspaper. Promising 'to report the nation to Canberra and Canberra to the nation', *The Australian* started life in 1964. What marked it apart from Murdoch's other ventures of the time was that it was a broadsheet with a heavier agenda (as well as a greater capacity to lose money). And, firmly on its agenda was political power. *The Australian* placed Murdoch at the center of power. He became a national figure. Though the newspaper lost money for years (broadsheet equals unpopular in Murdoch's terminology) it made a mark.

By the late 1960s, Murdoch's Australian interests were many and varied. He began to look further afield. The first international deal which shaped the media image of Murdoch was the purchase of the British Sunday newspaper, the *News of the World* in 1969. The *News of the World* was downmarket and addictively populist long before Murdoch entered the newspaper business. It was not known as 'The news of the screws' for nothing.

The *News of the World* was only the starter. It was a Sunday newspaper. The archaic inefficiency of Fleet Street meant that the presses remained silent during the week. It made obvious sense to use them.

And so, Murdoch rolled out a brash new form of populist journalism with the purchase for less than £500,000 of another British newspaper, the *Sun*, in 1969. To some the *Sun* was – and still is – the summation of all that is wrong with Murdoch. It is resolutely downmarket, famed for its Page Three topless models, pithy tastelessness, gung-ho nationalism and insatiable interest in the comings and goings of the stars.

The British do not have a monopoly on such things. Others followed. Among them was the *New York Post* bought by Murdoch in 1976. His relationship with the *Post* has been a typically complex saga. He lost control of it in 1988 – because he bought a local TV station, WNYW – and then regained control in 1993 when the newspaper was acquired once again by News Corp.

In 1981, Murdoch marked a remarkable new chapter in his career when he bought *The Times*, fighting off bids from the newspaper's editor (William Rees-Mogg) and a group of journalists, as well as from the editor of the *Sunday Times*, Harold Evans, and the inevitable Robert Maxwell. The 'top people's paper' was an unlikely bedfellow for the *Sun*. Indeed, with its court circulars and overbearing sense of tradition, *The Times* was an unlikely bedfellow for any other newspaper. There were predictable gasps of amazement when Murdoch, the downmarket populist, bought the bastion of English journalism. There were various pronouncements of impending doom and elderly clergymen turned the pages with new excitement, anticipating the arrival of their very own Page Three girl.

The purchase of *The Times* marked another important threshold in Murdoch's career. It was, after all, the newspaper of the Establishment which Murdoch expressed his distaste for. Then Murdoch found himself waging war on behalf of the Establishment.

Murdoch's newspapers in the UK were profitable. But, with growing interests elsewhere, he was keen to maximize their profit potential. Cash cows have to be milked. Blocking his path were the undoubtedly outdated processes and unions of Fleet Street. Demarcations and closed shops meant that the unions had a stranglehold on how and where newspapers were produced. Proprietors had gone along with these arrangements for decades. (It should not be forgotten that they, too, were culpable for the resulting inefficiencies and extravagances.) Murdoch drove a bulldozer through them.

In Wapping, in the east of London, he built a new printing plant which didn't need union labor. Computers were installed which meant that editorial content could be transferred directly to the page. On January 25th 1986 four million newspapers were produced at Wapping. This precipitated war.

Over the following months, Wapping became a battlefield. Thousands of pickets, from the print unions and others, attempted to bring printing at the plant to an end. The protests were increasingly violent and raged throughout most of 1996. The end result was complete victory for Murdoch. The printers were paid off with £60 million and disappeared into history. Murdoch was left with a massively more efficient operation and substantially reduced costs. Valuations of News Corp soared from $300 million to $1 billion.

Murdoch's confrontation with the unions was a defining moment in his career, the history of the unions and of Britain in the 1980s. It was also the defining moment in the public's perception of Murdoch. He was shown to be decisive and ruthless, someone who got what they wanted. He was clearly not only a powerful man but someone who was intent on using his power to create a business empire.

There is a feeling of opportunism about Murdoch's career. There is nothing wrong with that. Indeed, you could argue that he has remained close to his newspaper roots. But what is truly distinctive is the strategic energy he brought. Never standing still is a useful strategy in business and the boxing ring. During the 1980s, Murdoch created his empire. Acquisition followed acquisition. His aspirations appeared ever bolder. In 1985 he acquired Fox Studios; seven Metromedia TV stations followed in 1986; and, in 1988, he paid Walter Annenberg $3.2 billion for *TV Guide*.

The spending flurry was impressive but it was built on a mountain of debt. The beginning of the 1990s marked a watershed. News Corp's fabulous debts nearly brought it to its knees. Only a last-minute deal at the beginning of 1991 reportedly saved Murdoch's empire from ignominious collapse.

Undaunted, Murdoch has refused to stand still. As strategies go, it is among the most difficult to emulate or compete against.

Diss advantage #30

At the heart of strategy à la Michael Porter is the idea of competitive advantage. In the halcyon days of the 1960s and 1970s, such advantages always had a hint of permanence. Companies got ahead and stayed there.

And then, skeptical academics and more challenging times provided a new take on the notion of competitive advantage. Leading the charge was Richard D'Aveni. To D'Aveni, corporate survival was bound up with a series of 'dynamic strategic interactions'. Firms made their strategic moves only to have them countered by competitors, to which the firm sought a different advantage, and was countered once more – and so on. This was the world of h ypercompetition – an environment where advantages are rapidly created and eroded.

As D'Aveni wrote in *Hypercompetition: Managing the Dynamics of Strategic Maneuvering*:

> Advantages last only until competitors have duplicated or outmanoeuvred them … protecting advantages has become increasingly difficult. Once the advantage is copied or overcome, it is no longer an advantage. It is now a cost of doing business. Ultimately the innovator will only be able to exploit its advantage for a limited period of time before its competitors launch a counterattack. With the launch of this counterattack, the original advantage begins to erode, and a new initiative is needed.

The strategic goal of organizations in the hypercompetitive world, says D'Aveni, is to 'seize the initiative through creating a series of temporary advantages'. Organizations keep ahead of competitors by a perpetual leapfrogging from one temporary advantage to the next, creating new advantages and eroding those advantages held by competitors as they go.

The concept of hypercompetition came about because of a vacation D'Aveni took in Cape Cod:

> A hurricane came along called Hurricane Bob. While I was there it knocked out all the electricity for about four days. When the electricity came back on CNN was running a program on the fall of the Soviet Union. I had no idea that something like that could happen in a few days. It was one of the most important, economic, and political changes of our generation.
>
> So I stepped back and said to myself, I'm teaching all of these students about long-term plans and consistent strategies, how do you really do that in a world where significant earth shattering changes appear overnight? How do you do that when, even if you had all the resources of the Central Intelligence Agency, you still couldn't figure out that it was going to happen? I thought to myself, I must be a fraud, and decided to sit down and write a book that was about unsustainable advantages in an unpredictable world, rather than the traditional view of strategy.

D'Aveni reflects that 'the world has become even crazier since 1994, it's really hypercompetition on steroids today'.

Others are also taking aim at the central premise of Porterian strategic logic. Rita McGrath is a professor at Columbia University Graduate School of Business. Like D'Aveni, she argues that the days of sustainable competitive advantage are numbered.

Before executives head for the hills in fright, there is some reassurance from McGrath:

> There are still pockets of the economy where you can find the sustainable advantage. So if you take Rolls Royce or Steinway pianos or something like that, they're niche businesses where the brand really matters or the customers are super loyal or, businesses like

> Boeing where it's just really, really hard to build airplanes. So I still think there are places where you can find sustainable advantage and the traditional tools I would say work pretty well in those places. But we have to grapple with the fact that less and less of the economy is represented by those kinds of industries, with those kinds of characteristics.

McGrath is the author of *The End of Competitive Advantage: How to Keep Your Strategy Moving as Fast As Your Business* (2013). In an earlier book, *Discovery-Driven Growth*, McGrath explores how businesses can pursue dynamic growth, and encourage innovative new ventures without jeopardizing the enterprise through undue risk taking. She provides tools and processes to allow businesses to successfully exploit their opportunities. In *The End of Competitive Advantage*, she goes further:

> Well, if you think about the models and frameworks that had an impact on the field in the last 20 or 30 years, what's really new? We've had a lot of reliance on frameworks from the past that worked for a different era. I can't think of anything that's really had a big impact in the last 20 years. And I think that's because we're still looking for this mythical thing called a sustainable competitive advantage, and if you can't find one of those then what do you do?

And if competitive advantage is no longer sustainable then we really are talking about redefining the whole nature of strategy, aren't we? McGrath nods in agreement:

> Getting rid of the sustainable concept does redefine the entire competitive landscape. And I think what we're going to see in the future is firms that succeed over the long run are going to be really good at finding ideas, developing those ideas into business concepts, launching those business concepts, doing the exploitation thing, which is what strategy was always all about, but then also disengaging. And where I think firms need to change is to develop both the front end, the innovation incubation launch base, as well as the back end, the disengagement phase.

> And so what you're going to be seeing is almost as though they're surfing through these waves of advantage. You'll have one wave come and then it goes away, another wave come and then it goes away. And firms that are good at surging competitive advantage are going to be OK with that.

It is truly hypercompetition on steroids.

How to execute #31

Antonio Nieto-Rodriguez (antonionietorodriguez.com) is the world's leading champion of project management. He is Director of the Program Management Office at GlaxoSmithKline Vaccines and chair of the Project Management Institute. He is author of the best-selling *The Focused Organization*.

When he is running workshops with senior management teams, Antonio asks them to take turns listing their company's top three initiatives on a flipchart. No matter where he is in the world, the responses include more than three initiatives – often far more than three. Then he shares the list with the whole team. 'When I reveal the list, there is a moment of silence in the room and a certain embarrassment. If the executives of the firm do not know the company's priorities and are unable to focus on what is key, then they cannot expect this focus from their employees,' he told us.

Nieto-Rodriguez believes this lack of focus can also be explained by the pressure on many CEOs to show results quickly. Consequently, they often invest in many initiatives, thinking that they will increase their chances of success. The more balls you have in the air, the more you will catch. Right?

Well, no, actually. As Antonio points out, the reality is that human beings tend to be unfocused. A Harvard University study reported that at any given time 50 percent of the population is unfocused. Half of a company's staff are not focused on their work. The study also showed that those people who were focused on their tasks were happier than those who were unfocused. Whatever people were doing, whether it was working or reading or shopping, they tended to be happier if they focused on the activity instead of thinking about something else.

'The fact is that nature tends to disorder, and that being focused requires discipline, order, energy and effort. We humans have mixed feelings about expending energy, even if we know it will bring us pleasure,' says Nieto-Rodriguez. His work suggests a solution based on FOCUSED as a useful acronym:

F – Fewer projects, rather than many. A focused organization that is able to effectively select and prioritize its projects and invest in just one or two good initiatives at a time clearly outperforms organizations that take on too many projects. The few projects that are selected are linked to one or several strategic objectives and are fully supported by top management.

O – Organized staff. In a focused enterprise, the staff is organized in such a way that all personnel know what is expected of them. They do not waste time on activities that are not part of their core skill set; rather, they focus on their key strengths and core capabilities instead of trying all the time to improve their weaknesses.

C – Competitive mindset. The focused company competes with the outside world rather than internally. Internal competition, which is so negative in the long term, is eliminated because all of the organization's effort is placed on doing what it does best. The CEO and top management explicitly identify rival organizations, often referring to them in their speeches and communications to the company.

U – Urgency. Creating a sense of urgency is a competitive advantage. Urgency is also needed to focus people and encourage them to give their best performance.

S – Strategic alignment. Every initiative should be linked to one or several strategic objectives. Any initiative that is not so linked should be immediately cancelled. This alignment is necessary to ensure that the company achieves its stated goals.

E – Excellence. A focused organization applies the highest standards to everything it does, and its products and/or services are known for their quality. Sustainable excellence requires attention to the details of every aspect of the organization: values, quality of employees, internal and external processes, products, and customer service.

D – Discipline. Discipline should not be seen as something negative that inhibits innovation. Rather, innovation depends on discipline. Companies should clearly distinguish between the time set aside for creativity and time allocated to strategy execution. Focused organizations are able to make this distinction and to move from the creative phase to the execution phase very quickly. If companies spend too much on innovation, they will be too late by the time they decide to execute their strategy. The challenge for the CEO and the company's entire management team is to find the right balance between discipline and creativity/flexibility.

For Antonio Nieto-Rodriguez, focus is the route to successful strategic execution:

> The benefits of becoming a focused organization are significant and varied. Everybody in the focused organization, from the CEO to the accounts payable employee, knows the direction in which the organization is going, which two to three initiatives are the most important for that year, and the business case for these few critical initiatives. And the benefits can appear very quickly on the company's bottom line, particularly on the cost side. Costs are reduced when irrelevant projects are cancelled, which can add up to huge savings. There are many more likely benefits. The question is whether your organization can continue to ignore them.

But what does this look like in practice? An exemplar of the merits of focus was Jack Welch when he was CEO of General Electric.

By the end of the 1980s GE was a leaner and fitter organization after a healthy dose of downsizing instigated by Welch. Any complacency which may have existed had been eradicated. In retrospect, Welch's greatest decision may have been to go in with all guns blazing. Dramatic, though relatively short-lived change, was preferable to incremental change. 'Shun the incremental and go for the leap', was Welch's advice. No half measures.

Having proved that he could tear the company apart, Welch had to move onto the second stage: rebuilding a company fit for the twenty-first century. The hardware had been taken care of. Now came the software. Again, focus was the key.

Central to this was the concept of Work-Out which was launched in 1989. This came about, it is reputed, after Professor Kirby Warren of Columbia University asked Welch: 'Now that you have gotten so many people out of the organization, when are you going to get some of the work out?' At this stage 100,000 people had left GE. Welch liked the idea of getting the work out. The idea turned into a reality. With typical gusto, Welch brought in twenty or so business school professors and consultants to help turn the emergent concept into reality. Welch has called Work-out, 'a relentless, endless company-wide search for a better way to do everything we do'.

Work-out was a communication tool which offered GE employees a dramatic opportunity to change their working lives. In *Jack Welch Speaks* Janet Lowe explains:

> The idea was to hold a three-day, informal town meeting with 40 to 100 employees from all ranks of GE. The boss kicked things off by reviewing the business and laying out the agenda, then he or she left. The employees broke into groups, and aided by a facilitator, attacked separate parts of the problem. At the end, the boss returned to hear the proposed solutions. The boss had only three options: The idea could be accepted on the spot; rejected on the spot; or more information could be requested. If the boss asked for more information, he had to name a team and set a deadline for making a decision.

Work-out was astonishingly successful. It helped begin the process of rebuilding the bonds of trust between GE employees and management.

It gave employees a channel through which they could talk about what concerned them at work and then to actually change the way things were done. It broke down barriers. The gales of destruction were past. Creativity was in the air.

Welch the destroyer became Welch the empowerer. Work-out was part of a systematic opening up of GE. Walls between departments and functions came tumbling down. Middle management layers had been stripped away in the 1980s. With Work-out, Welch was enabling and encouraging GE people to talk to each other, work together and share information and experience. At first surprised, they soon reveled in the opportunity. GE's 1997 Annual Report noted:

> Strategic thinking rarely occurs spontaneously.
>
> **Michael Porter**

> In the early 1990s, after we had finished defining ourselves as a company of boundaryless people with a thirst for learning and a compulsion to share, it became unthinkable for any of us to tolerate – much less hire or promote – the tyrant, the turf defender, the autocrat, the big shot. They were simply yesterday.

Work-Out worked. In 1981 as Jack Welch began life as CEO, GE had total assets of $20 billion and revenues of $27.24 billion. Its earnings were $1.65 billion. With 440,000 employees worldwide, GE had a market value of $12 billion. By 1997, GE's total assets had mushroomed to $272.4 billion and total revenues to $79.18 billion. Around 260,000 employees – down a staggering 180,000 – produced earnings of $7.3 billion and gave the company a market value of $200 billion.

Welch moved from arch destroyer, corporate enemy number one, to potent creator. 'The most acclaimed SOB of the last decade is the most acclaimed CEO of this one,' announced *Industry Week* in 1994. The corporate demon king of the eighties was transformed into the role model for twenty-first century management. 'The two greatest corporate leaders of this century are Alfred Sloan of General Motors and Jack Welch of GE. And Welch would be the greater of the two because he set a new, contemporary paradigm for the corporation that is the model for the twenty-first century,' says the University of Michigan's Noel Tichy, a long-time observer of the Welch managerial style.

Focus is unrelenting. Work-Out didn't bring Welch's revolution at GE to an end. The next stage was the introduction of a wide-ranging quality program. Entitled Six Sigma, it was launched at the end of 1995. 'Six Sigma has spread like wildfire across the company, and it is transforming everything we do,' the company reported two years on.

People were the bread and butter of Jack Welch's managerial style. People matter – or were made to feel as though they matter. Said Welch: 'We are betting everything on our people – empowering them, giving them resources, and getting out of their way.'

Welch invested in people firstly by simply spending time with them. He calculated that he spent around half of his time with GE people, getting to know them, talking to them about their problems and, yes, no doubt berating them if performances were down. It was calculated that he knew around 1,000 people by name with a good idea of their job responsibilities.

And Jack Welch wanted the best people. He wanted to recruit them and retain them because it was good for his business:

> The reality is, we simply cannot afford to field anything but teams of A players. What is an A? At the leadership level, an A is a man or woman with a vision and the ability to articulate that vision to the team, so vividly and powerfully that it also becomes their vision. An A leader has enormous personal energy and, beyond that, the ability to energize others and draw out their best, usually on a global basis. An A leader has edge as well: the instinct and the courage to make the tough calls – decisively, but with fairness and absolute integrity.

And, clearly, Welch expected people to perform. He insisted that rewards packages were geared to individual as well as corporate achievements and ensured that rewards were carefully monitored and differentiated from business to business and person to person. The message was that if you win we all win.

Resources

Janet Lowe, *Jack Welch Speaks*, John Wiley, 1998.
Charles R. Day and Polly LaBarre, 'GE: Just your average everyday $60 billion family grocery store', *Industry Week*, 2 May 1994.
John Byrne, 'How Jack Welch runs GE', *Business Week*, 8 June 1998.
Antonio Nieto Rodriguez, *The Focused Organization*, Gower, 2012.

Cluster logic #32

Anker Boye is the charismatic Mayor of Odense, Denmark's third largest city. It is a city in transition. 'The City of Odense is rethinking itself from a city based on traditional industry to a city based on technology and knowledge,' says Boye.

With a population of 190,000 Odense is situated at the heart of Denmark. The city has a long tradition at being at the forefront of ideas. An English Benedictine monk, Aelnoth, based at the city's St. Knud's Monastery wrote Denmark's first literary work in 1100 and, in 1482, a German printer, Johan Snell, printed the first two books in Denmark at the invitation of Odense's clergy. The city is still best known as the birthplace of Hans Christian Andersen.

Today, the University of Southern Denmark, the broadcaster TV2, and more than 80 innovative companies in the robotic, component, integration and automation sectors are based in Odense, now the world's third largest hub in the robotics industry. Over the next 10 to 15 years, it is planned that investments totaling €4.5 billion will transform Odense into an internationally renowned city of knowledge.

It now appears natural for regions and cities such as Odense to specialize in certain types of activity. Knowledge and experience can be pooled, as can natural resources. Think of the Industrial Revolution in England and the cluster of textile companies in Lancashire and Yorkshire. Such was the level of specialization here that an entire town – Darwen in Lancashire – was dedicated to making loincloths for India. Of course, when the Indians started making their own loincloths, the town virtually ground to a halt overnight.

The decision taken at Miletus in Ancient Greece (around 500 BC) to specialize in wool and associated products may have been one of the earliest examples of regional specialization. Now, of course, we have Silicon Valley, Silicon Glen, Silicon Fen and various other regions identified with particular industries.

> Strategy doesn't come from a calendar-driven process; it isn't the product of a systematic search for ways of earning above average profits; strategy comes from viewing the world in new ways. Strategy starts with an ability to think in new and unconventional ways.
>
> **Gary Hamel**

Research by Harvard Business School's Michael Porter has examined the role of such areas in national competitiveness. Porter's research initially covered ten countries: the UK, Denmark, Italy, Japan, Korea, Singapore, Sweden, Switzerland, the US and Germany (then West Germany). Porter has since extended his study to include Japan, India, Canada, New Zealand, Portugal and the state of Massachusetts.

Porter sought to examine what makes a nation's firms and industries competitive in global markets and what propels a whole nation's economy to advance. He asked:

> Why are firms based in a particular nation able to create and sustain competitive advantage against the world's best competitors in a particular field? And why is one nation often the home for so many of an industry's world leaders. Why is tiny Switzerland the home base for international leaders in pharmaceuticals, chocolate and trading? Why are leaders in heavy trucks and mining equipment based in Sweden?

Porter returned to first principles – but not to Miletus:

> The principal economic goal of a nation is to produce a high and rising standard of living for its citizens. The ability to do so depends not on the amorphous notion of 'competitiveness' but on the

> productivity with which a nation's resources (labor and capital) are employed. Productivity is the prime determinant in the long run of a nation's standard of living.

Porter identified a central paradox. It is a paradox which confirms the management wisdom of the ancient Greeks. Companies and industries have become globalized and more international in their scope and aspirations than ever before. This, on the surface at least, would appear to suggest that the nation has lost its role in the international success of its firms:

> Companies, at first glance, seem to have transcended countries. Yet what I have learned in this study contradicts this conclusion. While globalization of competition might appear to make the nation less important, instead it seems to make it more so. With fewer impediments to trade to shelter uncompetitive domestic firms and industries, the home nation takes on growing significance because it is the source of the skills and technology that underpin competitive advantage.

Porter concluded that it is the intensity of domestic competition which often fuels success on a global stage.

Using Porter's work, the decision taken in Miletus would have been driven by factor conditions (these once would have included natural resources and plentiful supplies of labor; now they embrace data communications, university research and the availability of scientists, engineers or experts in a particular field); demand conditions (if there is strong national demand for a product or service this can give the industry a headstart in global competition); related and supporting industries (industries which are strong in particular countries are often surrounded by successful related industries); and firm strategy, structure and rivalry – domestic competition fuels growth and competitive strength.

How to succeed with strategy #33

Think again about competitive advantage

The argument about whether competitive advantage is sustainable or even possible is a passionate one. Roger Martin provides practical advice:

> I think a lot of the debate is not all that helpful. It is obvious that competitive advantage exists in the world. It is also obvious that competitive advantage doesn't last forever. Nothing lasts forever. And if you're trying to say that there is no such thing as competitive advantage, think of all the high performing, normally profitable companies, who've maintained that for years and years and years. It's hard to say that's not competitive advantage.
>
> So the question, to me, becomes, is there a thinking process that can help managers make decisions that produce advantage, to create high amounts of value for customers that enables you to make an attractive return, and opens up other possibilities to keep on renewing that? That's the fundamental question I ask. My view is, yes, there's a process of thinking that's more likely to get you answers. There's an intelligent process for identifying where to play, how to win, and if we make choices of that sort we will position ourselves in a way that gives us the opportunity to keep modifying that and enhancing it ahead of other people, so that we do have an

advantage over a sustained period of time. It's not the same advantage, right; it actually could be different sorts of advantages over time. So if you look over a 50-year period, it may actually be a whole bunch of different sorts of advantages. But it's because we have a practice of asking a set of questions that keeps us ahead of the game, rather than simply reacting to changes.

The world isn't static. Strategy isn't static, but that doesn't mean there isn't a way of thinking about the fundamental questions in a way that keeps you ahead of the competition.

Tune in

Says Richard Rumelt:

> Despite the roar of voices wanting to equate strategy with ambition, leadership, 'vision', planning, or the economic logic of competition, strategy is none of these. The core of strategy work is always the same: discovering the critical factors in a situation and designing a way of co-ordinating and focusing actions to deal with those factors.

Ask questions

You tune-in by asking questions. Simple. Advises Henry Mintzberg:

> We need to ask better questions and generate fewer hypotheses – to allow ourselves to be pulled by real-life concerns rather than pushed by reified concepts. We need better practice, not neater theory. So we must concern ourselves with process and content, statics and dynamics, constraint and inspiration, the cognitive and the collective, the planned and the learned, the economic and the political. In other words, we must give more attention to the entire elephant – to strategy formation as a whole. We may never see it fully, but we can certainly see it better.

Understand the broader context

David Bach of Yale School of Management observes:

> Companies are very comfortable with the idea that you can shape customers' expectations, erect entry barriers, change your relationship with suppliers, and mold your market environment. They are not so comfortable with the idea of trying to mold their social and political environment.

Think of barriers to exit not barriers to entry

In the past the strategic talk was of barriers to entry, but now we've got to start thinking in terms of barriers to exit. Says Rita McGrath:

> I argue that one of the things firms are going to do differently is they're going to be much more careful about sinking lots of assets and lots of investment into specifically competitive places because if you need to move fast you don't want a lot of fixed assets. You want to be able to use assets that are fairly fungible. It's access to assets rather than ownership of assets, which we're going to see as the defining issue in how you expend resources going forward.

Look to create new markets

Mining existing markets is necessary but is increasingly insufficient to secure future growth. Says *Blue Ocean Strategy* co-author Renée Mauborgne:

> The challenge is to create new demand, what we call market space. New market space is about creating a company's future. Companies can continue to mine their wealth from an existing market space – that's maintenance. They can concentrate on market share. But there is something more – the act of creation. Creating new market space will become increasingly vital.

Creating new market space provides growth. There are two paths to growth. One is the mergers and acquisition path, which often leads to growth but rarely leads to profitable growth. The other is organic growth by creating new businesses. While this path is profitable and necessary, in markets where supply exceeds demand, companies are often hesitant because they don't have a path forward to believe that they could succeed in changing things. They need a bridge to get there. Hopefully, some of the ideas and analytics we have been developing will help companies in building that bridge.

Involve as many people as possible

The C-suite doesn't have a monopoly on strategic wisdom – or any other kind of wisdom. People throughout an organization need to be emboldened to think and care about strategy. Says Roger Martin:

> Wherever you are in the organization you have to make strategy choices too. If everybody felt that they have to make strategy choices I think corporations would work a lot better than saying we make the choices up above, and you people down there execute. It's not the way the world actually works, and it's not a helpful kind of conception of the corporation.

Know yourself

Leaders are encouraged to really understand their inner ambitions and motivations. Much the same applies to organizations. Success comes from within. Chris Zook of Bain told us that the consistent revelation of his research and case studies is that the main barrier to companies finding their next wave of growth is themselves:

> The answer is internal. Only 15 percent of the variation in performance among companies is related to choice of market, and 85

percent is related to how those businesses compete against others around them. And when we actually look at the main issues and barriers that companies have in that regard, we find more of them tend to be internal than external. Businesses can tend to be their own enemies, and self-awareness, at the end of the day, is probably at the epicenter of a lot of the great success stories and great failure stories in business.

Look inside.

About the authors

Des Dearlove and Stuart Crainer create and champion business ideas. They are the creators of the Thinkers50 (www.thinkers50.com) – the original global ranking of business thought leaders. Their work in this area led *Management Today* to describe them as 'market makers par excellence.'

As business commentators, Stuart and Des have been asking difficult questions for over two decades. Now, they help organizations come up with their own wicked questions and explore how best to engage with people and communicate the answers. They were advisors to the 2009 British Government report on employee engagement and are adjunct professors at IE Business School in Madrid. Their clients include Swarovski, Cisco, the Department of Economic Development in Abu Dhabi, Fujitsu, and Heidrick & Struggles.

Stuart and Des are former columnists to *The Times* (London), contributing editors to the American magazine *Strategy+Business*, and editors of the best-selling *Financial Times Handbook of Management*. Their books include *The Management Century*, *Gravy Training*, *The Future of Leadership*, and *Generation Entrepreneur*. They are available in more than twenty languages.

Stuart was editor of the award-winning magazine *Business Strategy Review*. Des is an associate fellow of Saïd Business School at Oxford University and is the author of a best-selling study of the leadership style of Richard Branson.

Des and Stuart have taught MBA students, professors and senior executives on programmes all over the world. These include the Oxford Strategic Leadership Programme at the Saïd Business School at Oxford University; Columbia Business School in New York; the Tuck Business School at Dartmouth College in New Hampshire; IMD in Lausanne, Switzerland; and London Business School.

They also advise organizations and leaders on how best to identify and communicate their key messages. Their clients in this sphere include some of the world's leading business schools.

Index